# The Wheel of
# Engaged Buddhism

# The Wheel of

# Engaged Buddhism

## A New Map of the Path

BY KENNETH KRAFT

*illustrations by J.C. Brown*

New York   WEATHERHILL   Tokyo

*First edition, 1999*

Published by Weatherhill, Inc.

Printed in the United States
Cataloging-in-Publication Data available from the Library of Congress.

# CONTENTS

# Introduction

THE PROCESS OF SPIRITUAL AWAKENING has long been experienced and described as a path. In Buddhism, awakening depends largely on one's own efforts, versus reliance on a divine being. Just as past behavior has decisively affected present circumstances, present behavior decisively shapes the future. A result of this emphasis on self-effort is that paths and path theories are more developed in Buddhism than in other world religions or native traditions. Shakyamuni Buddha set forth the "noble eight-fold path," a course of authentic understanding, conduct, and meditation. In the centuries that followed, other paths were proposed. One elaborate blueprint systematized types of religious aspirants, techniques of spiritual practice, meditative states, and all the realms of the Buddhist cosmos.

The Sanskrit word for spiritual path, *mārga*, has many related meanings that testify to the richness of the concept: way, road, path, course, channel, passage, mode, method, style, direction, right way, search, inquiry. The Chinese word for spiritual path, *tao*—and its Japanese equivalent, *dō*—have even greater breadth. Depending on context, *tao* can indicate an ordinary road, a social discipline, a martial art, or reality itself. When we are on the Way, does a life journey enfold a spiritual journey, or does a spiritual journey enfold a life journey? Ultimately, they are not two.

As eras shifted, and as Buddhism moved from one culture to another, paths were transformed accordingly. Indian Buddhists, with religious imaginations that favored the grand and cosmic, characteristically framed paths in terms of numerous lifetimes. According to one calculation, attainment of full Buddhahood would require $384 \times 10^{58}$ years of diligent self-cultivation. However, this seemed a bit extreme to Buddhists in other cultures, who deftly shaved eons off the process. By the time Buddhism became established in Japan, masters declared that Buddhahood could be achieved in one's present life "in this very body."

The process of reconnoitering spiritual paths continues today, as exemplified by recent developments in engaged Buddhism. Briefly, engaged Buddhism is an international movement whose participants seek to apply the Buddhist ideals of wisdom and compassion to present-day social, political, and environmental issues. Although Buddhism has typically given priority to the spiritual liberation of the individual, engaged Buddhists look for ways to expand the notion of spiritual liberation to other arenas (without abandoning the essential role of individual enlightenment). How might awakening be interpreted in social and political terms, to embrace families, nations, or all people? How can it be interpreted in environmental terms, to embrace animals, plants, or ecosystems? Just to be able to discuss such possibilities requires new language. Some recent coinages are thought-provoking even without their definitions: a culture of awakening, the politics of enlightenment, enlightened society, ecological awakening, eco-karma.

Indian Buddhists once asked, How do I leave the world? Contemporary Buddhists ask, How do I heal the world? If I cannot responsibly leave the world, how do I follow a spiritual path *in* the world? Such questions lead to new forms of practice. For example, ordinary activities are reframed as conducive to spiritual development. In East Asia, Zen monks have long viewed manual labor as a vital aspect of training and an expression of insight. There is no spiritual affair loftier than "carrying water and gathering wood." In the West today, comparably mundane activities include grocery shopping, studying, driving to work, and so on. Can such tasks be transformed by the alchemy of intention and awareness into modes of self-realization and compassionate service?

Zen teacher Robert Aitken, in a recent book, composed a series of four-line verses based on everyday situations. Each poem, in the form of a vow, serves as a reminder to practice more deeply. An appendix of nearly three hundred "occasions for practice" confirms the inclusive spirit of the enterprise: indexed entries range from "check my face in the mirror" and "nastiness" to "car keys" and "tire blows out." This approach departs from the Indian Buddhist view that mundane existence is a form of bondage. While some schools of Buddhism advocate a single type of practice as sufficient and all-encompassing, Aitken and other engaged Buddhists assert that in today's world, spiritual practice needs to be flexible, diverse, and inventive.

Engaged Buddhism entails both inner and outer work. We must change the world, we must change ourselves, and we must change ourselves in order to change the world. Awareness and compassionate action reinforce each other. In a letter to fellow practitioners, two Dutch Buddhist activists write:

> We are learning how necessary personal development is for social change. The great ideologies have not survived and cannot take us into the new century. When we think of the world as something we can change without changing ourselves, we will not go very far.

By the same token, an exclusively inner transformation, however profound, is not the end of the trail. Greed, anger, and delusion—known as the "three poisons" in Buddhism—need to be uprooted in personal lives, but they also have to be dealt with as social and political realities. Throughout the world today, large-scale systems cause suffering as surely as psychological factors cause suffering. Traditional Buddhism focused on the latter; engaged Buddhism focuses on both.

Buddhist activists value engagement not only as a potential contribution to the world, but also as a potential instrument of personal development. "Social action is itself a kind of meditation and can be a great ripener of compassion and equanimity," writes Zen teacher Philip Kapleau. A corollary goes a step further: wisdom is not authentic unless expressed in action. Before enlightenment, an old Buddhist metaphor maintains, one's inherent Buddha nature is like a mirror in a box. For engaged Buddhists, the same image applies to awakening in relation to the world: a mirror functions fully and freely only when it is out of the box. Contemporary Buddhists are therefore looking for models of spirituality that go beyond the solitary meditator. The spiritual quest is not about a fixed self getting some thing called enlightenment. "It may even be that the knower, the actor, the 'unit' of enlightenment, is not the single person," activist Donald Rothberg suggests.

Although Buddhist tradition has handed down bountiful descriptions of predominantly inner paths, there are few comparable maps of spiritually motivated involvement in the world. Initially, many people assume that the "outer" realms are sufficiently visible and familiar not to require a map. Yet, for those who seek a modern, this-worldly spirituality, the signposts seem scattered, and guidelines are far from self-evident. As Robert Aitken has acknowledged, "This is a step beyond the monastery walls, uncharted by the old teachers. . . . Not an easy path, certainly." Given the differences between past and present Buddhists—differences of historical context, religious imagination, and meaningful modes of practice—a new map may be helpful.

Pictorial representations of paths are as old as Buddhism: according to tradition, Shakyamuni envisioned the first such image as the Wheel of Life. Painting, sculpture, architecture, and other media have long been used to illustrate significant aspects of various paths. One of the strongest advocates of religious art was the Japanese monk Kūkai (774–835), founder of a sect that endures today. For Kūkai, iconography promoted spiritual growth:

The Dharma has no speech, but without speech it cannot be expressed. Eternal truth transcends color, but only by means of color can it be understood. . . . The various attitudes and *mudrās* [gestures] of the holy images all have their source in Buddha's love, and one may attain Buddhahood at the sight of them. Thus the secrets of the sutras and commentaries can be depicted in art, and the essential truths of the esoteric teaching are all set forth therein. Neither teachers nor students can dispense with it. Art is what reveals to us the state of perfection.

Several illustrations of Buddhist paths continue to serve as sources of insight and inspiration. The Wheel of Life is known throughout Asia and is especially prominent in Tibet. Doubling as a map of the path and a map of the cosmos, this richly colorful diagram teems with a cast of ordinary and extraordinary beings. A central area depicts six realms of conditioned existence *(samsāra)*, populated by gods, fighting titans, humans, animals, hungry ghosts, and denizens of hell. The border of the Wheel illustrates the doctrine of dependent origination, in twelve links that lead from ignorance to death. Shakyamuni or a bodhisattva sometimes appears in the pictorial space outside the Wheel, because the highest aim for aspirants on this path is to free oneself from the cycle of samsaric existence. An East Asian variant of the Wheel of Life adds four paths of enlightenment to the six realms, eliminates the twelve links, and puts the Sino-Japanese character for "mind" in the Wheel's hub.

Another influential depiction of a path is the Ten Oxherding Pictures. Developed in the eleventh century by the Ch'an (Zen) school in China, this series of ten images uses an ox to symbolize Buddha nature, inherent and universal. The spiritual aspirant, represented by a young oxherd, is shown searching for the ox, finding it, taming it, and eventually, in the tenth image, returning to society. In contrast to the colorful style of the Wheel of Life, the Oxherding Pictures usually employ a spare black-and-white style, framing the ten images in identical circles. The eighth illustration, entitled "Both Self and Ox Forgotten," is a completely empty circle. Generations of Zen practitioners have felt special fondness for the set's third picture, in which the searching figure first glimpses the partially hidden ox, because that scene corresponds to an initial experience of awakening (*kenshō* in Japanese).

A third pictorial map, still used in Tibetan teaching, illustrates the meditative Path of Calm. A man, an elephant, and a monkey are repeatedly depicted on an ascending road with sharp curves. The man represents the meditator, the elephant symbolizes the mind, and the monkey stands for the mind's agitation. At the outset, the monkey leads the elephant, and the man pursues them from a distance. Eventually, the man gains control over the elephant, and the monkey disappears. The ever-increasing stillness of mind (*śamatha*) is also expressed through the use of black and white: the elephant and the monkey start out completely black, but their blackness recedes in each successive scene until both animals are completely white. The Path of Calm and the Oxherding Pictures probably have historical links. In terms of basic structure, these three maps employ distinctly different patterns: a circle with multiple sectors, a flat line with directional movement, and an ascending line that zigzags.

The Wheel of Engaged Buddhism proposed here began with a single idea: I happened to think of the Ten Oxherding Pictures in conjunction with an essay I was writing on Buddhist activism. In the essay I made the following suggestion: "Maybe today's socially engaged Buddhists will develop another set of Ten Oxherding Pictures as a sequel or companion to the first, illuminating the progressive stages of practice in the world." I was hoping that someone wiser and more qualified than myself might become interested in such a project. Alas, silence. So I began to experiment, initially by consulting art books in the library for images that expressed aspects of contemporary engaged practice. The Wheel attained its present form by fits and starts, aided by valuable contributions from colleagues, friends, and students.

How well must a cartographer know the terrain in order to produce an accurate and useful map? It depends. In certain situations, the mapmaker must be intimately familiar with the territory. In other cases, it may be enough to sketch a coastline or identify a pattern of topography. Many maps of spiritual paths claim to record only the actual experiences of practitioners, though most of them go on to describe advanced states theoretically accessible to the most gifted and highly trained devotees. The paths depicted visually in the Wheel of Engaged Buddhism, and verbally in the text, are based almost entirely on the experience of contemporary Buddhists. When ideals are expressed, they are polestars by which one may set one's course, not all-or-nothing absolutes. The investigation of a path can bear fruit well before that path has been mastered.

There is one ideal that consistently undergirds engaged Buddhism, and that is the notion of a bodhisattva. *Bodhi* means "awaken," and *sattva* means "being." A bodhisattva can be an awakened being, a being on the way to awakening, or a being who awakens others. Bodhisattvas share one overriding aspiration: to become a Buddha; and they share one overriding motivation: to relieve others' suffering. Shakyamuni was a bodhisattva before he became a Buddha. Traditionally, the time he spent in this role includes not only the period of austerities and meditation that preceded his enlightenment, but also his many previous lives, as popularly depicted in the Jataka tales. There are also archetypal, cosmic bodhisattvas such as Manjushri, who embodies wisdom, and Avalokiteshvara (Chinese: Kuan-yin), who embodies compassion. In some streams of Buddhism, practitioners are called bodhisattvas. The path for a bodhisattva-in-training classically has ten stages: joy, immaculacy, splendor, brilliance, invincibility, immediacy, transcendence, immovability, eminence, and "dharma-cloud." Such heroic terms were meant to inspire rather than exclude; this path has room for beginner bodhisattvas too. Thus a bodhisattva is both a paragon and a paradigm, an exemplar for individual conduct and a gateway to an entire worldview.

The bodhisattva ideal is freshly evocative today, for Buddhists and non-Buddhists alike. Philip Kapleau captures the gist of it in nonsectarian terms: "The object of gaining an insight into the inner truth of things is really to qualify oneself for greater compassionate action in the world." In this book, I use the phrase *bodhisattva mind* to refer to the deep intention to come to awakening together with all beings. (It is not a traditional term, though it is closely related to several.) At once ordinary and mysterious, bodhisattva mind sometimes manifests as a quality of awareness, sometimes as a mode of practice.

The *New York Times* recently asked a number of scholars what they thought was the "most underrated idea." One answered, "Kindness." Engaged Buddhists would agree. The Dalai Lama makes it official when he says, "My religion is kindness." Basically, the Wheel of Engaged Buddhism is a mandala of kind gestures. Although a mandala is not a maze or labyrinth, it wouldn't hurt to have a strong thread as a guarantee that we will not lose the way. That thread is kindness.

# Navigating the Wheel

A WHEEL is one of the oldest symbols in Buddhism. The eight-spoked Wheel of Dharma is an emblem of the teachings that flowed from Shakyamuni's enlightenment. The Wheel of Life, described in the Introduction, also has ancient roots. In Zen, a circle, complete in itself, without beginning or end, symbolizes ultimate oneness. Buddhism is not alone, of course, in recognizing the metaphorical resonance of wheels and circles:

> The turning wheel is a powerful symbol of the mystery at the heart of life. Planets and solar systems and electrons in their orbits are wheels revolving within larger wheels, just as the hours and seasons of day and year rotate too, and the circulation of the blood in the body, and the vast hydrological cycles that sustain our living world. Like the sacred hoop of the Native Americans and the round dances and mandalas of ancient peoples, the wheel reminds us that all is alive and moving, interconnected and intersecting.

Mandalas, circular diagrams of symbolic forms, have played many roles in Buddhism. In the main, mandalas are seen as blueprints for spiritual practice that leads eventually to liberation. The most ambitious mandalas are cosmograms, intended to represent not only the highest states of consciousness but also the entire universe. In the influential Diamond

World mandala, which contains 1,461 Buddhas and bodhisattvas, compassion is supposed to radiate outward from the center, while wisdom spirals inward toward the center. Mandalas have been used over the centuries as objects of meditation, teaching devices, vehicles of initiation, and prayers for others' welfare. There are majestic mandalas in stone, such as Borobudur in Java, and half-forgotten geographic mandalas, such as the Kunisaki Peninsula in Japan. Traditionally, to make a mandala is itself a form of meditation.

The structure of the illustrated Wheel of Engaged Buddhism is comparatively simple. There are ten sectors. The image in each sector symbolizes a path of engaged/spiritual practice. Each path has a title. Locations in the Wheel are as follows, starting at the center:

Moving into the World . . . . . . . . . . . . . . . . . . . . . . . . . . . . . hub
Cultivating Awareness in Daily Life . . . . . . . . . . . . . . . . . first ring
Embracing Family . . . . . . . . . . . . . . . . . . second ring, upper right
Working with Others . . . . . . . . . . . . . . . second ring, lower right
Participating in Politics . . . . . . . . . . . . . . second ring, lower left
Caring for the Earth . . . . . . . . . . . . . . . . second ring, upper left
Extending Compassionate Action . . . . . . . . . . . . . third ring, top
Exploring New Terrain . . . . . . . . . . . . . . . . . . third ring, right
At Ease Amid Activity . . . . . . . . . . . . . . . . . third ring, bottom
Spreading Joy in Ten Directions . . . . . . . . . . . . . third ring, left

The ten paths are meant to be suggestive rather than exhaustive. Each path is actually an untold number of paths, as individuals and groups in different circumstances find their own way. In the Wheel, five of the paths are primarily *fields* of practice (cultivating awareness in daily life, embracing family, working with others, participating in politics, caring for the Earth). The other five paths are primarily *modes* of practice (moving into the world, extending compassionate action, exploring new terrain, at ease amid activity, and spreading joy in ten directions). A wheel format makes it possible to envision ten paths simultaneously, give them equal weight, and consider their mutual relatedness.

Hand gestures (*mudrās*) are used in Buddhism as symbols of spiritual ideas and teachings. Some of the traditional *mudrās* are relatively straightforward: if a flat open hand (fingers together) faces downward, it means generosity; if it faces upward, it means the act of teaching. Many two-handed *mudrās* are more complex: a fist grasping an upright index finger, thumbs tucked in, symbolizes the perfect interpenetration of form and emptiness. In the Wheel, various hand gestures represent specific paths. As sign language, they are allusive but not elusive; the Wheel is meant to be handy—useful and accessible. The changing hand positions also help to give the Wheel a sense of motion. Engaged Buddhism, a movement itself, embraces movement into the world.

Flowers have figured prominently in Buddhist art and literature for thousands of years, in their own right and as symbols. The titles of a number of Buddhist sutras refer to flowers because those texts claim to represent the flower (peak) of Buddhist insight. One of the best known is the *Sutra of the Lotus of the Wonderful Law*, or the *Lotus Sutra*. Lotus flowers often connote enlightenment amid the pain and dust of the world: though a lotus plant has its roots in the mud at the bottom of a pond, above the water it puts forth beautiful lush blossoms, perfect just as they are.

In the Wheel, the lotus flower does more than adorn. It refers to the process of awakening, which sometimes takes its course the way a flower blossoms, one petal unfolding after another. For some people, the flower may correspond to the search for insight; for others, it may signify the actualization of insight, and the quest for ever-deeper enlightenment. Since engaged Buddhists believe that awakening is actualized in the realm of self-*and-others*, the lotus doubles as a symbol of bodhisattva mind. Can we press one more load on these frail petals? If so, a flower is a felicitous reminder of interdependence. As Thich Nhat Hanh observes,

> A flower is always receiving non-flower elements like water, air, and sunshine, and it is always giving something to the universe.

A flower is a stream of change, and a person is also a stream of change. At every instant, there is input and output. When we look deeply at the flower, we see that it is always being born and always dying, and that it is not independent of other things. The components of the universe depend on one another for their existence.

In short, the lotus flower expresses the awareness that engaged Buddhists strive to bring to their involvement in the world.

All of the Wheel's paths are linked to one another. Each path can be seen as part of a meaningful sequence, and each path has dimensions that go beyond any sequence. For example, the Wheel's second ring is composed of four sectors, representing engagement in family, work, politics, and the environment. While this particular sequence may reflect widening spheres of involvement (according to customary standards), all four paths are nonetheless equal in significance and value. The path of household practice is potentially as boundless as any other. The larger individual images that accompany each essay create an alternative arrangement, a variation which can stand on its own. The gradual blossoming of the lotus flower in these images validates the possibility of advancement. For some people, linearity keeps things orderly and marks progress. For others, linearity is . . . too linear. Here it is not necessary to choose: the Wheel format preserves the advantages of nonlinearity, while the individual images show how the ten paths can be arranged sequentially.

A visual model with balanced sectors and recognizable images may give a first impression of clarity and ease, as if the paths of engaged spirituality were fully mapped and evident to all. On the contrary, engaged Buddhism is in a period of experimentation, when it is more valuable to pose questions than to settle them. Buddhists do not minimize the difficulty of engaged practice. Cultivating awareness in daily life can be hard, working with others can be hard, caring for the Earth can be hard, and so on. There are many points along the way where one feels completely stymied. Readers familiar with Zen koans (profoundly challenging spiritual conundrums) will recognize that each path has koan-like aspects. In order to grasp the heart of a path, one has to find some way to get inside it. When meaningful solutions are found, on the path and in the world, they most often come not from thinking dispassionately about matters but from entering into each situation fully and authentically.

One can gain entrance to the Wheel at any point, just as one can begin reading a map at any point. Each of the ten paths is fit to serve as "the first." With familiarity, the number of possible applications increases. A fruitful exercise is to try to find one's own place in the Wheel, the way outdoor community maps indicate "You are here." A particular path may amply express the current thrust of one's efforts. Or perhaps some combination of two or more paths may reflect one's present priorities in a useful way. For example, a teacher in an inner-city school may find that the two paths of working with others and extending compassionate action, in combination, illuminate salient aspects of her engaged practice. Alternatively, the Wheel can highlight neglected areas of our lives that invite more attention, and suggest new ways to expand practice in those areas. One may also use the Wheel to clarify future goals, or to see how elements of practice and fields of engagement have changed over time.

In every culture in which Buddhism has found a home, it has presented itself as a practical religion. In that spirit, the essays contain exercises, guided meditations, and suggested actions consonant with the path under discussion. Give these a try, as circumstances permit. All are accessible to nonspecialists, though some may call for more than a one-time commitment. Engaging with the exercises in this book will yield experiences and insights beyond what reading alone can provide. Take the Wheel for a spin.

Wherever the paths of engaged Buddhism may lead, there will be opportunities to actualize bodhisattva mind. Sometimes, after traveling for a while on an unfamiliar road or trail, we unexpectedly come to a place that we know well. Having thought that we were exploring, maybe even lost, we exclaim, "Oh, I know where *this* is!" It happens in other ways, too. At the end of *The Wizard of Oz*, Dorothy wakes up and realizes that she is home after all, and in fact has never left. Such experiences are metaphors for spiritual awakening. On the paths of engaged Buddhism, we are not searching for some exotic foreign land, some far-distant realm of enlightenment. Rather, we are going deeper into our own lives, "back to where we all belong," until we stumble upon that placeless place that is our true home. Zen teacher and veteran trekker Peter Matthiessen says it this way:

> To glimpse one's own true nature is a kind of homecoming, to a place East of the Sun, West of the Moon—the homegoing that needs no home, like that waterfall on the upper Suli Gad that turns to mist before touching the Earth and rises once again into the sky.

ACCORDING TO TRADITION, the young prince Shakyamuni slipped away from his sheltered life in the palace and beheld, one after another, a sick person, an old person, a dead person, and a monk. Each of these encounters was a profound shock. The first three "signs" brought Shakyamuni face-to-face with suffering. In the demeanor of the monk, Shakyamuni recognized the possibility of transcending suffering.

Ordinarily, to take the first steps on a spiritual path is to leave the world in some way. That is the point of monasticism, which provides institutional support for withdrawal. For laypeople as well, the early phases of a spiritual quest are typically directed inward. Yet all religions also offer teachings and practices that lead to a reintegration of spiritual and worldly life. One valid pattern is to find a path back into the world at a later, more mature stage of spiritual development.

The story of Shakyamuni's exposure to suffering is archetypal because it happens so often: deeply felt pain, one's own or others' or both, is the most common precipitant of spiritual searching. The yearning to alleviate suffering is at the same time a seed of engagement. A contemporary Zen practitioner, Vanya Palmers, recalls a specific incident that sparked a change in his life:

It was a picture that first triggered my interest in animal rights. It showed a monkey in a "restraining chair," immobilized in the technical surroundings of screws, wires, and plexiglass. My one-year-old daughter probably had something to do with the fact that this picture grabbed me. In the frightened, confused face of the monkey, I saw—not just with my eyes but with my heart and body—the face of my daughter.

Palmers went on to develop campaigns for animal rights in Europe and North America. Another engaged Buddhist, John Seed, reports a comparable experience:

Somehow I found myself involved in what turned out to be the first direct action in Australia—or in the world for that matter—in defense of the rain forests. All of a sudden, the forest was inside me and was calling to me, and it was the most powerful thing I have ever felt.

Seed is now head of an international organization that works to protect rain forests. One need not be a spiritual adept to be intensely affected by suffering; there are people who recall realizations they had as children, even before they could conceptualize their understanding.

In Mahayana Buddhism, a tradition that shuns absolutes, the closest thing to an absolute is compassion. The Dalai Lama makes this point unequivocally: "The root of all Buddhist teaching is compassion. . . . The Buddha who teaches these doctrines is even said to be born from compassion. The chief quality of a Buddha is great compassion." The prerequisite for this path on the Wheel, "moving into the world," is none other than *being moved* to enter the world. As Buddhist scholar Robert Thurman writes, "A beginner bodhisattva need not be very advanced in enlightenment, merely firmly dedicated to universal love and compassion."

Bodhisattva mind is the aspiration to awaken, to help others, and to help others awaken. The intention to do so is sometimes roused without conscious effort; in other cases, teachers encourage self-inquiry:

What are the roots of my own caring action? What have we to offer one another to alleviate suffering? How do we *begin* to act compassionately for change? Especially, how do we begin those actions for change that may not happen naturally and spontaneously?

The point of entry cannot be taken for granted. Once, when I was visiting an English castle, I was handed a portable audio tape that was supposed to provide a guided tour of the sprawling premises. For some reason, I was unable to locate the very first site on the tour, and as a result the entire tape became useless. When one *does* find a starting point, and takes a first step, one crosses a threshold. Is it stepping out, or stepping in?

A practice that dovetails with this path is walking meditation. Mindful walking is an accessible introductory discipline, an actual experience of intentional movement, and a clear indication that practice continues off the meditation cushion. It is especially effective outdoors in a natural setting with a group. Thich Nhat Hanh offers the following guidelines:

> Choose a nice road for your practice, along the shore of a river, in a park, on the flat roof of a building, in the woods, or along a bamboo fence. Such places are ideal, but they are not essential. I know there are people who practice walking meditation in reformation camps, even in small prison cells.
> It is best if the road is not too rough or too steep. Slow down and concentrate on your steps. Be aware of each move. Walk straight ahead with dignity, calm, and comfort. Consciously make an imprint on the ground as you step. Walk as the Buddha would.

Another practice that reflects the spirit of this path is a meditation conducive to the cultivation of loving kindness (*mettā*). The basic instructions are straightforward. After taking a seated position in which you are comfortable yet alert, use the breath or a comparable method to quiet the mind. Mentally repeat the following phrases, savoring their meaning: *May I be happy. May I be well. May I be peaceful and at ease. May I be filled with loving kindness.* When you feel ready, direct these compassionate thoughts to another person, perhaps a parent or beloved family member. Picture that person and recite the same phrases: *May she be happy. May she be well.* . . . In this manner, the exercise can be extended indefinitely. Vipassana meditation teacher Jack Kornfield advises:

> You can gradually begin to include others: friends, community members, neighbors, people everywhere, animals, the whole Earth, and all beings. Then you can even experiment with including the most difficult people in your life, wishing that they, too, be filled with loving kindness and peace.

To feel the depth of one's own compassion is itself a blessing.

A crucial shift occurs when the desire to relieve suffering becomes a firm resolve to do so. In Mahayana Buddhism, resolute practitioners take four bodhisattva vows. Today, formal vows may seem quaint or fanatical, but true vows are more than ceremonial promises; they have transformative power. The first bodhisattva vow is: "All beings, without number, I vow to liberate." This bold declaration means many things; in the context of engaged Buddhism, it signifies an unbounded commitment to practice compassion. Any worthy aspiration can be kneaded into a homemade vow. Robert Aitken does this by composing short verses, such as:

> Waking up in the morning
>    I vow with all beings
> to be ready for sparks of the Dharma
> from flowers or children or birds.

The mandalic image in the hub of the Wheel symbolizes the genesis of an engaged spirituality. Since compassion and commitment must arise or be aroused repeatedly, the spirit of this path permeates all others. Buddhist activist Fran Peavey reports that after many years of involvement, she still asks herself the same basic questions: "For the past fifteen years, most mornings I have sat and meditated and asked myself what I could do to help the world. What is the work of today and what is the work of this time?" In the Wheel, all forms of service and work for social change become potential vehicles of bodhisattva practice. If you think, "Somebody ought to do something about that," that somebody might be you. A student once asked Thich Nhat Hanh, "There are so many urgent problems. What should I do?" He replied, "Take one thing and do it very deeply and carefully, and you will be doing everything at the same time." In this sense, the path of moving into the world broadcasts a question, and each of the surrounding paths in the Wheel proposes an answer to that question.

One of the fundamental tenets of Buddhism is that everything in the universe is interconnected and interdependent. Actions and thoughts have repercussions far beyond the immediate and the familiar. Although we may speak of moving into the world, from the standpoint of interdependence the distinction between self and world becomes transparent. We can't run after the world, and we can't run away from the world. Other conventional distinctions also collapse. The journey "out" becomes a continuation and a deepening of the journey "in." Work on behalf of others and work on oneself become one. "We can, of course, help through all that we *do*," one participant writes. "But at the deepest level we help through who we *are*. . . . We work on ourselves, then, in order to help others. And we help others as a vehicle for working on ourselves." Practice and engagement are two sides of the same coin. Both could be called practice; both could be called engagement. Victoria Kieburtz, a doctor, mother, and senior Zen student, concludes:

> Practice is bodhisattvic, whether we intend it to be or not, and the aim or purpose of practice, as much as we can talk about an aim or a purpose, is to alleviate suffering. In fact, the drive to realize one's true nature is the same as the drive to alleviate suffering. Even going further, the alleviation of suffering is the flowering of our true nature.

## Cultivating Awareness
## in Daily Life

ONE OF THE MAIN TENETS of engaged Buddhism is that the domain of everyday life and the domain of spiritual development are not, in essence, separate. Almost any activity, no matter how "ordinary," can be approached in the spirit of engaged practice, as an opportunity for the cultivation of awareness, selflessness, and compassion.

This is not a new teaching. More than a thousand years ago, in the Ch'an (Zen) monasteries of China, farming and manual labor were recast as religious practice. Carrying water could equal seated meditation as a form of training; gathering wood could equal a wise sermon as an expression of spiritual insight. The thirteenth-century Japanese Zen master Dōgen stated this principle in terms of the Dharma: "Those who see worldly life as an obstacle to Dharma see no Dharma in everyday actions; they have not yet discovered that there are no everyday actions outside of Dharma."

When the nitty-gritty terrain of ordinary experience seems too far removed from the promised fruits of spiritual life, we yearn for ways to bridge the gap. Yesterday was scattered, today is slipping away, tomorrow there are countless things to be done. Is it possible to experience clarity and calm amid the commotion of everyday activity? The titles of several recent books testify to our longing to touch the transcendent within the mundane:

*Everyday Zen*
*Start Where You Are*
*Wherever You Go, There You Are*
*Peace Is Every Step*
*Present Moment, Wonderful Moment*
*Liberation in the Palm of Your Hand*

The practice that epitomizes the path of awareness in daily life is mindfulness. Common to all streams of Buddhism, mindfulness combines wholehearted involvement in the here-and-now, steady attentiveness to the task at hand, and a tolerant openness to the elements of inner and outer experience. Zen master Ikkyū, in fifteenth-century Japan, thrust this advice at a questioner:

> One day a man of the people said to Zen master Ikkyū, "Master, will you please write for me some maxims of the highest wisdom?" Ikkyū immediately took his brush and wrote the word: "Attention."
>
> "Is that all?" asked the man. "Will you not add something more?" Ikkyū then wrote twice running: "Attention. Attention."
>
> "Well," remarked the man rather irritably, "I really don't see much depth or subtlety in what you have just written." Then Ikkyū wrote the same word three times running: "Attention. Attention. Attention."
>
> Half-angered, the man demanded, "What does that word 'attention' mean anyway?" Ikkyū answered gently, "Attention means attention."

Ikkyū's determined repetition of the word "attention" is a demonstration that reinforces his point, because true attentiveness is sustained, not sporadic. What we know of Ikkyū's life adds a dimension to this anecdote that is pertinent for engaged Buddhists. Though a monk, Ikkyū deliberately immersed himself in the world, so his own practice of mindfulness did not depend on the disciplined atmosphere of a monastery.

Mindfulness is a fitting practice for a newcomer, but this first practice is also a lifetime discipline for novices and adepts alike. Zen teachers use eating as an example. When we eat, we usually do something else at the same time: talk with friends or family, watch television, read, listen to music, and so on. Or we become lost in thought about something completely unrelated to the eating. Then we wonder why we become hungry again so soon after a meal. As an exercise in mindfulness, perhaps when alone, try to *just eat*. To do this, one puts aside all other activities and becomes completely absorbed in the eating: slowing down, picking up a fork with full attention, chewing each mouthful deliberately.

The Wheel's image for this path, a hand holding a glass, stands for any activity performed mindfully. The practice of attention does not require solitude, the refined atmosphere of a Japanese tea ceremony, or any other special conditions. Is an ordinary glass of juice too humble to express the grandeur and gravity of the Way? Not at all. The highest truth is nowhere else than in that glass, and nowhere juicier. Japan's greatest haiku poet, Bashō, repeatedly demonstrated the true spirit of mindfulness practice. Compelled one night to sleep in a stable, he did not fail to pay attention:

> Fleas, lice,
> the horse pissing
> near my pillow.

But what is the link between attentiveness and engagement? Does this path belong in a Wheel of *Engaged* Buddhism? Yes, for several reasons. Alert involvement in ordinary activities is itself a meaningful expression of engagement, even in the absence of overt participation in broader social, political, or environmental work. When one is mindful, one is less likely to cause harm and more likely to recognize others' needs. Engagement *without* attentiveness can be unskillful and even harmful. One practitioner connects mindfulness and bodhisattva mind in the following way:

> When I get depressed, off course, tangled in my engaged Buddhist practice, it helps me to flash on the bodhisattva vows, specifically to say to myself, kind of like a Zen hit: "SAVE ALL BEINGS

RIGHT NOW!" Which brings me back to whatever it is I *can* do right in *this* moment. Often it is just to be mindful and meticulous and here now, washing the dishes or folding my clothes.

Folding clothes peacefully contributes to peace on a much larger scale. In the Wheel, the path of daily awareness touches five other paths; in reality, this path is integral to all other paths.

Heightened attentiveness is not the whole of it, however. The cultivation of awareness also involves sensitivity to the moral implications of behavior, our own behavior especially. When I and fellow baby boomers were first attracted to Buddhist practice, many of us accepted the traditional Buddhist precepts but did not give them much further thought (what a relief, in meditation, not to have to think about anything or anybody!). Yet Buddhism has always identified moral conduct as one of the three foundations of spiritual training, as indispensable as meditation and insight. The five cardinal precepts are: do not kill, steal, have improper sex, lie, or take intoxicants. Today, Thich Nhat Hanh calls these precepts "mindfulness trainings" and restates them in positive terms. The above list becomes reverence for life, generosity, sexual responsibility, deep listening and loving speech, and diet for a mindful society.

There are many ways to work with the five precepts as mindfulness trainings. One teacher suggests the following: Pick a precept, negatively or positively phrased. Find a well-defined form of self-discipline that reflects the spirit of the chosen precept. Then follow that practice for a full week. For example, to carry out generosity, resolve to give freely of your time to those who need it. As an exercise in loving speech, decide not to gossip. Or, in the spirit of the fifth precept, vow to avoid unmindful consumption of magazines, television, and movies. If such exercises are undertaken with sincerity, something changes right away, and perseverance for even a limited time yields lasting discoveries.

One of the abiding challenges of daily practice is that it is not always clear what the proper object or scope of awareness should be. In formal meditation, the focus is intentionally circumscribed (the breath is often used in this way). But amid ordinary activity, especially in a world as complex as ours, vexing questions arise. For example, is it enough to use electricity sparingly, when a fifth of our electricity comes from power plants that breed nuclear waste? If the drink in the glass happens to be a Coke, other considerations may come into play. Many of us know something about the global marketing of Coca-Cola. Economist Juliet Schor describes how poor people are induced to spend their few pesos on soft drinks and fast food rather than more nutritious fare, a process that can lead to illness and malnutrition. Should that information be part of our awareness if we are about to drink a Coke?

Once when environmentalist Stephanie Kaza was practicing walking meditation outdoors during a retreat, she heard loud gear-grinding noises in the distance and recognized the sound of a logging truck. A lover of trees, she felt waves of alarm, helplessness, and grief. She also questioned herself about the role of mindfulness practice:

> *The forests! The forests!* . . . I struggle with this slow walking, torn between acting and not acting. It seems like an indulgence to take the time to cultivate mindfulness when so much is being lost.
>
> But this is the tension—to find a considered way of acting not based on reaction. Building a different kind of sanity requires a stable base for careful action. It means being willing to know all the dimensions of the reality of destruction, being willing to breathe with the tension of emotional response, being willing to cultivate tolerance for unresolved conflict. This nonverbal form of ethical deliberation depends on the careful work of paying attention to the whole thing.

Adepts in martial arts report that as they advance in skill, their peripheral vision also improves. In a similar way, mindfulness can always be broadened and deepened, whatever the circumstances.

"Be here now" seems straightforward enough, at first. At the moment I am aware of fingers clicking on keyboard, pressure of buttocks on seat, thoughts jostling about, and so on. Yet the present moment also shields a mystery in its heart. What does it really mean to enter deeply into the present? Are we able to see *through* the present to the timeless? Although language hits its limits here, the ultimate "object" of true awareness is Buddha nature itself, or any equivalent term for Reality. The pissing horse let Bashō in on this secret, and Bashō kindly shared it with us.

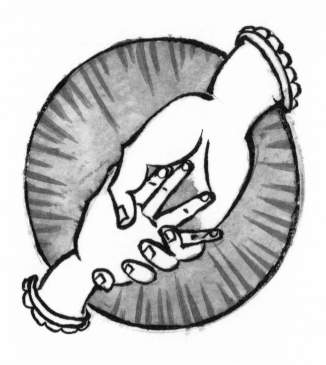

# Embracing Family

THE IMAGE FOR THIS PATH in the Wheel portrays an adult and a child holding hands. Changing a diaper, sitting with an ill parent, working through a disagreement with a spouse — these and comparable activities are valid ways to practice engaged Buddhism. At home, the ancient ideals of wisdom and compassion are none other than understanding and love. Bodhisattva mind is expressed as selflessness, the willingness to put aside one's own needs for the sake of others.

Family life as a path of practice is a relatively undeveloped notion in traditional Buddhist texts. Certain devotional activities, ethical precepts, and the like were recommended for householders, and laypeople played important roles in the religious life of Buddhist communities, yet the monastic path was almost always considered the highest calling. Shakyamuni *left* his family, including his wife and just-born son, to seek enlightenment. Some accounts of the young prince's departure add a poignant detail: he wanted to get at least a glimpse of his new son, but when he peered into the women's quarters, his sleeping wife's arm obscured the baby's face. (Years later, Shakyamuni's wife, son, and foster mother are said to have joined his religious community.) In East Asia, the word for monastic ordination is composed of the two characters "leave" and "home." Zen master Dōgen claimed (at times) that only monks could reach enlightenment. In sculpture and painting, revered figures grasp bowls, ropes, mirrors, and many other things, but there is no mudra for holding the hand of another person.

In mainstream Western culture today, monasticism is not widely supported, so most aspiring Buddhists must find other viable approaches. How does one practice *within* a family? Is it possible to treat the home as a *dōjo*, a place of training in the Way? If so, what is lost—or gained? Although the word "family" often implies a conventional nuclear family, here it is meant to include all kinds of families, conventional or not. Nor does family-as-path imply a rejection of the solitary aspects of spiritual development.

When family becomes a living *dōjo*, new dimensions of Buddhist teachings are illuminated. Buddhism holds that, on an absolute level, we are one with all existence, inseparably linked to a farmer in Indonesia and a fish in the depths of the ocean. Then how much more so are we connected to our parents, siblings, spouse, or children? This is surely the relative level. Just as the precepts can inform mindfulness, they can inform countless activities in a family setting. Reverence for life, generosity, sexual responsibility, loving speech, avoidance of intoxicants—simply listing them will bring vital examples to mind. Buddhist treatises on giving (*dāna*) analyze the eventual dissolution of boundaries between the helper and the helped; those same boundaries dissolve momentarily whenever a nurturing father puts a raincoat on his six-year-old daughter. Or consider the actuality of impermanence: in a family, everyone seems to be changing all the time.

Many people are exploring possible congruences between parenting and practice. The consensus so far: no easy matter! For example, a parent with access to formal training in a Buddhist community may yearn to participate in an intensive meditation retreat (*sesshin*) yet balk at leaving her children for a week. When the choice is to go on retreat (and proper child care is arranged), troubling questions continue to arise.

Victoria Kieburtz writes:

> With my own "suffering" diminished and the dust settled, I had
> fallen into a duality which identified the sufferers as outside
> myself, outside my *zazen* [meditation]. In order to help them, I had
> to be with them in real-time. How could I fulfill my duty to truly
> help anyone, other than myself, if I was isolated in sesshin? We are
> told that sesshin benefits beings on seen and unseen levels, but I
> failed to feel that in my bones. What I did feel was that my chil-
> dren were home for an endless week without me, and that my
> absence was a source of pain for them.

The obverse of this same dilemma, *not* attending retreats, is that it is a constant challenge to treat common household activities, on the scale of making beds or settling arguments, as a fully authentic path of awakening. "It
is as hard to get the children herded into the car pool and down the road
to the bus as it is to chant sutras in the Buddha hall on a cold morning,"
asserts poet-activist Gary Snyder (who has done both). "One move is not
better than the other."

Newly articulated practices and principles are often applicable
beyond Buddhist circles. "Part of your work as a parent is to keep growing
in self-knowledge and in awareness." "Try seeing the children as your
teachers." "Instead of sitting up all night in meditation, sit up all night
when the children are sick." In a monastery, a bell calls monks to meditation; in a home, a bell can call family members to mindfulness. A mother
in the San Francisco area reports that a household bell has become a natural part of family life:

> It lives on the altar in Jason's room, where anyone can get it at any
> time and bring it to sound anywhere in the house. Whenever the
> bell is sounded, we all stop whatever we are doing and breathe
> three times. Then we continue mindfully with what we were doing.
> Our bell has been sounded to greet new guests, on the way to the
> bathroom, in the midst of bustling dinner preparations, during
> meals, in the heat of arguments, and directly after angry outbursts.

Children can practice, seriously and playfully, in ways befitting their age. A very simple ritual at mealtime or bedtime may be enough for everyone involved. If a young child expresses an interest in meditation, suggest the "chrysanthemum" or "half-chrysanthemum" position (definition: any position you like). A twelve-year-old boy explains why he enjoys meditating: "It awakens my brain so I can think better." Some practices assume surprising forms when translated for children. For a teenager, being mindful may mean: When you are talking on the phone, *just talk on the phone*. Unexpected questions are bound to come up. "Mom, how do you fix the precepts once they're broken?"

Children find ways to deal with religious activities that do not feel natural to them. When young Dhyana Cabarga and her friend Audrey were included in events at a California Zen center, they began adding the word "not," sotto voce, to communal chants. The mealtime verses thus became:

> Innumerable labors did not bring us this food; we should *not*
>     know how it comes to us.
> Receiving this offering, we should *not* consider whether our
>     virtue and practice deserve it.
> *Not* desiring the natural order of mind, we should *not* be free
>     from greed, hate, and delusion.
> This food is *not* for the Three Treasures; it is *not* for our teachers,
>     family, and all beings.

Which is preferable, chanting "not" or not chanting? "Saying the chant this way was fun, and no one knew we were doing it," Dhyana recalls. "And we didn't know if our virtue and practice deserved it anyway."

Commitments to one's family and commitments beyond family must be adjusted and balanced all the time. Concern for the world's far-flung conflagrations does not justify neglect of the hearth close at hand. One teacher offers a useful self-check: "If you cannot serve your wife or husband or child or parent, how are you going to serve society?" Engaged Buddhism's insistence on systemic change does not overlook the vital role of a homemaker: a parent striving to raise children to be nonviolent and free of prejudice is thereby working to change society.

The family is where death is encountered most intimately and profoundly. Extending the familial spirit of tender care for the terminally ill, a number of American Buddhists have been drawn to hospice work. The best known are Joan Halifax, of the Upaya Foundation in Santa Fe, and the late Issan Dorsey, a Zen priest with a colorful past that included stints as a female impersonator. Dorsey became abbot of the Hartford Street Zen Center in San Francisco's largely gay Castro district just as the AIDS epidemic hit the area. His response to the suffering was spontaneous and courageous: "If your friends and students are dying, and in need of attention, you take them in." Dorsey himself succumbed to AIDS in 1990, but not before he had established Maitri Hospice next door to the Hartford Street Zen Center.

In premodern Asian cultures, to withdraw from family and society was often the most radical course available, proof of the ultimate urgency of one's spiritual search. Now, in a period of familial disintegration and social fragmentation, the most radical course may not be to abandon a family, but to embrace one.

# Working with Others

I N PRESENT-DAY AMERICA, the place of work can be as significant as the home in terms of essential relationships and self-fulfillment. Work is also one of the most important points of intersection with social systems and the environment. As Buddhists strive to integrate practice and work, they are asking: How does one earn a living honorably in a materialistic, acquisitive society? What does it mean to practice at work? How can I be kinder and more skillful in dealing with others? For those whose principal work is solitary or inside the home, much of the substance of this path still applies.

According to the concept of "right livelihood," from the original eightfold path enunciated by the Buddha, monks have not been permitted to engage in worldly pursuits. They receive their food as alms, and in some cultures they are literally forbidden to touch money. For laypeople, right livelihood originally stressed abstention from any occupation that harms living beings, such as slaughtering animals or selling weapons. Social thinker Theodore Roszak writes, "The Buddha, in his wisdom, made 'right livelihood' (another word, I think, for vocation) one of the steps to enlightenment." At first, Roszak's interpretation sounds oversimplified, but it prompts a closer look at possible links between vocation and awakening.

Today, even when harmful activities are avoided (to the best of one's knowledge), the personal, ethical, and economic issues are so complicated that it is no longer clear what qualifies as right livelihood. New definitions cite new criteria, such as work that provides personal fulfillment, serves other people, and makes a difference in the world. A key test is whether or not one's job accords with one's deepest intentions: the best kind of work is "on purpose." Still, questions remain. Are certain jobs simply immoral? Are the privileged obliged to use their privileges to help others? Which occupations adequately honor our responsibility to future generations? Is it wrong to want money?

Right livelihood is not just about *what* one does for a living, but also about *how* one does it. The foundation of practice on this path is to become one with your work, giving it your full energy and attention, the way a Zen monk is supposed to rake pebbles in a rock garden. One maxim simply states, "Do what needs to be done." Another goes further: "Zen isn't doing what you like to do, but liking what you have to do." At the beginning of an intensive meditation retreat, the master sometimes reminds the participants: "One person making a wholehearted effort will benefit the entire group, and one person who gives way to negative thoughts will pull the whole group down." In Japanese monasteries the constant give-and-take between monks is seen as an opportunity to build character and refine insight, the way stones grinding against one another at the foot of a waterfall are eventually polished smooth. Work, solitary or social, thus becomes a potential vehicle for spiritual self-cultivation. These teachings are equally valid in modern secular settings.

Many principles germane to the path of working with others are not, of course, distinctively Buddhist: be true to yourself, be thoughtful of others, keep your word, and so on. The Wheel's image of a handshake expresses several of these familiar tenets. We can also enlist the idea of a firm handshake to represent Zen's emphasis on becoming one with your work. Just as two hands become one handshake, self and task join to become just the doing.

Pace is another important aspect of work, as old Zen cooking manuals note. In the kitchen or out, some tasks must be done briskly, while others must not be rushed. An architect whose designs are socially and environmentally responsible may nonetheless fail to practice right livelihood if she takes on more work than she can handle. Chronically busy writer Sam Keen was once asked by his wife, "Would you be willing to be less efficient?"

New techniques are being devised as conditions change. An account of a harried physician offers an example. The doctor was suffering from various symptoms of stress, and had become a compulsive clock-watcher, when he had an idea:

> He walked over to his secretary's supply cabinet and pulled out a package of the little green dots used for color-coding the files. He placed one on his watch and decided that, since he couldn't stop watching the clock, he'd use the dot as a visual cue, a reminder to center himself by taking one conscious breath and dropping his shoulders. The next day he placed a dot on the wall clock . . . and by the end of the week had placed a green dot on each exam room door. A few weeks after initiating this workday practice, he said that, much to his own surprise, he had stopped, breathed, and relaxed one hundred times in a single day.

The green dots worked because the doctor found a method suited to his circumstances, and followed through sincerely.

An exercise: If you have a habit of leaping anxiously for the phone, let it ring while you take one mindful breath. Hard-core practitioners of "telephone meditation" breathe for three full rings before answering.

The five precepts are endlessly applicable in work situations. For example, the third precept, sexual responsibility, would prohibit sexual harassment and the use of sex to sell products. The fourth precept goes beyond not lying to embrace right speech. In the workplace, where verbal interaction is at the heart of things, speech can be an especially fruitful arena of practice. A recent version of the fourth precept, by Thich Nhat Hanh, takes the form of a vow:

> Aware of the suffering caused by unmindful speech and the inability to listen to others, I vow to cultivate loving speech and deep listening in order to bring joy and happiness to others and relieve others of their suffering. I vow to learn to speak truthfully, with words that inspire self-confidence, joy, and hope. I am determined not to spread news that I do not know to be certain and not to criticize or condemn things of which I am not sure. I will refrain from uttering words that can cause division or discord, or that can cause the family or the community to break. I will make all efforts to reconcile and resolve all conflicts, however small.

In one paragraph, enough to practice for a lifetime!

Working with others is often hard, and work as practice is often hard. Too often, the workplace becomes a battleground of power or a temple of "moneytheism." The business world poses special challenges for many contemporary Buddhists. Barry Keesan, a Zen practitioner who founded a company, reports: "Every day for many years I asked myself, 'Is business compatible with practice? Can it be done?'. . . I worked on this koan every day of my business career." On a fundamental level, Buddhism and capitalism seem incompatible: Buddhism seeks to restrain desires, while capitalism seeks to increase them. On one side, there is Gandhi, who declared, "There is enough for everyone's need, but not for everyone's greed." On the other side, there is Zsa Zsa Gabor, who explained, "A limousine is not an acquired taste. You get used to it immediately." The *modus operandi* of today's business world is Gaborian, not Gandhian.

Business has so far been largely oblivious to its effect on the environment. The businesses trying in earnest to operate ecologically represent just a tiny fraction of total commercial activity. Often, essential operations (such as trucking products to market) have the same effect on the environment whether the company is green or not. "There is no polite way to say that business is destroying the world," charges alternative economist Paul Hawken. In this light, issues of right livelihood acquire sharper edges.

Confronted with the faults and offenses of secular society, some religious groups prefer avoidance and insularity. That has been the strategy of the Amish and of Hasidic Jews, for example. Most Western Buddhists, in contrast, seek reform through engagement, even from within the belly of the beast. They are making determined efforts to bring spiritual awareness and values to the workplace, sometimes introducing the concept of right livelihood itself. According to Keesan:

> Here and there, in the midst of our muddy capitalist swamp, some lotuses are blossoming. I see other people taking risks, trying to change the rules of business. My belief is that there will be more and more people from all traditions accepting spirituality in the world of commerce and business. My experience has shown that people are hungry for this in an environment with so little joy. Business leaders, too, want something more. The world desperately needs this type of engaged practice.

Bodhisattvas aspire to work for all beings. The spirit of service is therefore a fitting expression of bodhisattva mind on this path, not only in working with others, but also in regard to the deepest meaning of work. Our work is ultimately a kind of offering. What do we have to offer? Our energy and attentiveness, our integrity and compassion. Zen teacher Norman Fischer reflects:

> We work hard because there is someone who requires it. Who is that someone? We can say all beings, we can say reality itself, we can say Buddha, but none of these is quite accurate. Someone requires it, and maybe it is best to say we don't know who that someone is. Why doesn't this person do it herself? Because we are her tools. Our body, our mind, and our whole life are her tools. So we throw ourselves into our work with a lot of verve and joy.

# Participating in Politics

FOR THE PAST DECADE, the leader of the democratic opposition in Burma, Aung San Suu Kyi, has been held prisoner in her home or placed under comparable restrictions by the ruling junta. In 1991, she was awarded the Nobel Peace Prize. "Tell us the difference between politics and meditation," an interviewer asked. Suu Kyi replied:

> Well, if you're meditating and a mosquito comes and bites you, you have to think, "Biting . . . biting . . . biting." And you are aware that the mosquito is biting and you just keep sitting there. You don't stop the mosquito and you don't try to shake it off.
>
> But politics is not like that. We try everything we can not to hurt others and create feelings of antipathy. But if people are doing things that are unacceptable to us as the party that represents the democratic movement, we can't just sit there and say, "They are doing it. . . . They are doing it. . . . They are doing it." And not do anything. For instance, they have been sentencing our people unjustly to prison. We're not going to meditate and say, "They've been unjust. . . ." We're going to do something.

In her simple statement, "We're going to do something," Aung San Suu Kyi speaks for many Buddhists who believe that one must participate actively in social and political affairs, and that such participation is not alien to Buddhism.

For most of Buddhism's long history, the domains of society, politics, and religion were inseparable. Though the monastic order founded by Shakyamuni rejected a number of social norms, the Sangha had considerable social impact. In the Asian cultures that were predominantly Buddhist, the influence of Buddhism was as pervasive as the influence of Christianity in medieval Europe. Today, most of the formerly Buddhist countries have been so affected by modernization and Westernization that they only offer glimpses of their traditional character. While few Buddhists would suggest that it is possible or desirable to return to a premodern alliance of sacred and secular, many are seeking constructive ways to actualize nonsectarian religious values in public life.

The Wheel's image, two hands releasing a dove, borrows an international symbol for peace. Nonviolence is a cornerstone of Buddhist thought and practice. The theme of peace is especially germane to the path of politics, but it also pertains to every path. Engaged Buddhism holds that inner peace, family peace, community peace, and world peace are deeply interconnected.

Like Aung San Suu Kyi, politically active Buddhists argue that one must be conversant with the important events and forces of the present day, and respond accordingly. In England, a meditation teacher campaigns for Parliament. In Thailand, Buddhist leaders speak out for democratic reform. In Sri Lanka, monks attempt to mediate between warring ethnic groups. In Massachusetts, a Vipassana meditator directs the Cambridge Peace Commission. In New York City, Zen students go on "street retreats" with the homeless. In San Francisco, volunteers plant gardens in former drug parks. The California-based Buddhist Peace Fellowship, founded "to bring a Buddhist perspective to the peace movement, and the peace movement to the Buddhist community," has over four thousand members in the United States and around the world. The International Network of Engaged Buddhists, based in Thailand, coordinates worldwide efforts on human rights, education, and alternative economics.

Central motifs are emerging in contemporary Buddhist social and political thought. Whatever Buddhism's past strengths and weaknesses in the political realm, today it is receptive to Western ideals such as democracy, human rights, activism for social change, and religion's independence from state power. Nonviolence continues to serve as a foundational principle, a touchstone for means and ends alike. The precepts, originally a code of conduct for individual monks, are now being applied to global concerns. Thus "do not kill" has been extended to include resistance to war and militarism; "do not steal" proscribes exploitative economic systems; and "do not lie" becomes an injunction to speak truth to those in power. Thich Nhat Hanh's "diet for a mindful society," an interpretation of the precept that restricts intoxicants, highlights the social grounds of individual conduct. As noted in the Introduction, Buddhism classically analyzed suffering in psychological and spiritual terms (desire is the principal cause of suffering). Present-day Buddhist thinkers maintain that social conditions and political institutions also affect suffering in crucial ways, exacerbating it or easing it. The same forces that were underscored in early Buddhism— desire, greed, anger, ignorance—must be dealt with socially and politically as well as individually. For example, runaway consumerism makes individuals anxious, widens the gap between rich and poor nationally and internationally, and wrecks the environment. Sulak Sivaraksa bluntly declares: "Consumer culture works hand-in-glove with greed and lust, arising out of delusion and ignorance."

The influential Thai monk Buddhadhāsa (1906–93) envisioned spiritually healthy alternatives to the reigning paradigm of economic growth and profit above all. In an attempt to extricate fair-minded principles of socialist theory from the abuses of state socialism, he called his stance "dhammic socialism." Buddhadhāsa's jungle monastery, where laypeople were also welcome, was conceived as a model of a community dedicated to awakening. The Dalai Lama has proposed that the Tibetan plateau become a "zone of peace," where people live free of conflict and in a sound ecological relationship with their surroundings. Whatever the discrepancy between the Dalai Lama's optimism and the current situation, his plan offers a Buddhist perspective on the prospects of social and political reform. Others speculate further. Buddhist writer Ken Jones, in Wales, imagines a day when excessively acquisitive or competitive behavior is regarded as an "antisocial hang-up, much like heavy drinking."

Current ruminations about the betterment of society are one area where engaged Buddhism departs noticeably from the antecedents offered by Buddhist tradition. In the past, social transformation was typically given up as a lost cause (versus individual transformation), so theoretical models of desirable societies are scarce. "Today, a bodhisattva should be a politician or even an economist," poet-activist Nanao Sakaki has said, only partly in jest. A Buddhist Marx may not be required, but a few Buddhists making their marks in economics and public policy would be edifying.

Like other spiritually motivated activists, engaged Buddhists try not to compromise the integrity of means in the service of ends. One of my colleagues likes to write letters to the editor, and he sees his letter writing as a form of engaged practice. Although many of the letters are prompted by anger at someone, he does not write a word until he has done a brief loving-kindness meditation that includes the object of his anger. How can contemplative practice contribute most effectively to social change? Donald Rothberg offers a nuanced view:

> Efforts to bring awareness and wisdom into relationships, families, communities, and work, while not always issuing in explicit efforts at social change or social service, nonetheless may provide much of the foundation for institutional change and larger-scale responses to suffering.

Thich Nhat Hanh goes so far as to claim that devotees "have to be working for peace in order to have peace in themselves." In this spirit, social action can be approached as a ripener of compassion, a furtherance of self-awareness, and a way of pursuing enlightenment.

The challenges and struggles on this path are acute. As awareness of the far-reaching repercussions of behavior deepens, perennial questions acquire new urgency: What is our responsibility? What is effective action? When do we fight (nonviolently), and when do we make peace? For over a decade, Cathy Hoffman, director of the Cambridge Peace Commission, has been building community in a diverse city. Yet sometimes her social activism and her meditation practice seem to prescribe different courses: "I feel a tension between creating programs that take the side of 'social justice' on the one hand, and taking a peacemaking role of trying to reconcile people with different points of view, on the other."

An apt expression of bodhisattva mind on this path is the resolve to respond to suffering wherever it may be found. The corresponding practice is not to close oneself to others' pain. "Find ways to be with those who are suffering, including personal contact, visits, images, and sounds," one teacher advises. The process can begin simply, in the way one reads a newspaper or watches television. When a news item is particularly sad or disturbing, put down the newspaper or turn off the television. Breathe deeply and consciously, taking in the bad news, allowing yourself to feel pain rather than pushing it away. For those who wish to go further in this direction, Tibetan teacher Sogyal Rinpoche offers a meditative exercise:

> In the moment you feel compassion welling up in you, don't brush it aside, don't shrug it off and try quickly to return to "normal." Don't be afraid of your feeling or embarrassed by it, or allow yourself to be distracted.... Be vulnerable: use that quick, bright uprush of compassion; focus on it, go deep into your heart and meditate on it.

In paintings of the Wheel of Life, there is often a small image of a bodhisattva, such as Kuan-yin, in each of the six realms. The idea is that bodhisattvas manage to be present in all realms, however hellish, in order to facilitate liberation. The dove can play a similar role here: not only does it represent the animal realm (where beings suffer), it also is free to fly off to any other path.

Is it possible to live justly in an unjust world? The question is like a Zen koan: one must struggle existentially rather than settle for an intellectual answer. The director of the Buddhist Peace Fellowship, Alan Senauke, has said: "Often I feel discouraged by the overwhelming tide of violence, nationalism, racism, and all painful divisions we create between and among us. But the work of kind words, nonviolence, mindful breaths, and quiet sitting has its own core of steel." Even in the bleakest inner-city ghetto or the most wretched refugee camp, the flower of awareness can blossom. Even with thousands of nuclear warheads still on alert, the dove of peace is eager to fly.

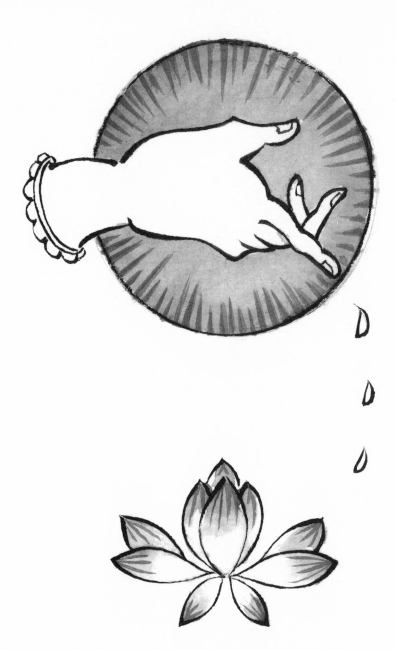

# Caring for the Earth

A THIRD OF THE WORLD'S PEOPLE do not have an adequate supply of clean water. Fifty thousand plant and animal species a year are lost to human predation, the greatest mass extinction in several hundred millennia. Forests continue to disappear around the globe. Most of us are aware that the planet is in serious trouble, and we search for meaningful ways to act in response. The path of caring for the Earth draws upon the resources of traditional Buddhism but also takes the tradition in new directions.

When the Dalai Lama accepted the Nobel Peace Prize in 1989, he explicitly called for environmental protection of the Tibetan plateau, citing the Buddhist principles of nonviolence and compassion for all beings. In Thailand, monks are "ordaining" trees to protect forests targeted for clear cutting. In the West, Buddhists in many walks of life are grappling with the ecocrisis personally and politically, using methods that range from self-restraint to organized group action.

One of the central teachings of Buddhism, as we have noted, is the reality of interdependence: everything depends on countless causes and conditions for its existence. Today, that ancient analysis seems remarkably pertinent to an understanding of ecosystems and environmental values. If the air I breathe depends on oxygen-producing forests, then those forests are as crucial to my health as my own lungs. In a way, those forests *are* my lungs. Some people experience this interdependence so deeply that, in the case of forests, they are able to imagine how things seem from the perspective of the trees. In current parlance, an ecological awakening leads to a greening of the self. What could be a stronger foundation for environmental activism?

Here, bodhisattva mind manifests as a heartfelt sense of oneness with other beings and the Earth. Zen students at the Green Gulch Zen Center in northern California have been struggling to save what remains of an old-growth redwood forest. After a recent demonstration, a member of the group was asked if she was going to return to the Zen Center for the next training period. "No," she replied. "I'm going to practice in the trees." Oneness with other life-forms is also expressed in less lofty ways. The medieval Japanese Zen monk Ryōkan was reportedly so considerate toward all beings that when he sunned himself in the morning he would carefully pick the lice out of his robe and place them on a nearby rock. After sunning himself, he would gently place the lice back in his robe.

The practices characteristic of this path, broadly speaking, are restraint and stewardship. Restraint grounded in ecological awareness means: being conscious of what one consumes; distinguishing between real needs and artificial desires; and finding ways to live more simply. Here is a critical point of intersection between ecology and economics. How much is enough? A maxim of the voluntary simplicity movement is "Live simply, so that others may simply live." If the meaning of "others" is expanded to include nonhumans, the adage still stands. Contrary to expectation, this kind of restraint is not a grim exercise in self-denial; the true spirit of "downshifting" has been captured on a bumper sticker: "Less consumption, more joy."

Stewardship is conduct that aims to protect humans, other creatures, and the Earth's resources. The watering of a plant, as depicted in the Wheel, is a down-to-earth example. One can be watering the seeds of awareness at the same time. At the Green Gulch Zen Center, in order to restore and protect the land, members plant trees annually, improve field soils by large-scale composting, cull non-native plants, and maintain a twenty-acre organic farm. A more complex and disturbing dilemma is the disposition of long-lived nuclear waste. That may require a form of stewardship that Buddhist teacher Joanna Macy calls "nuclear guardianship." Since it may not be possible to contain radioactive waste through technological means alone, Macy envisions an ongoing role for human guardians, a collective form of mindfulness that would have to be sustained generation after generation.

As we have seen elsewhere on the Wheel of Engaged Buddhism, meditative awareness can inform activism, and activism can intensify meditation. Australian John Seed, who defends rain forests, says:

> I think I developed some qualities in meditation that are very useful in environmental work, such as being able to focus on the process rather than the goal. . . . For every forest we save, we can't help but notice that a thousand forests disappear. So the sitting practice taught me how to work joyously without seeing any sweet fruits of my action.

Ancient Buddhist genres are being adapted to create ecologically oriented spiritual practices. An exercise taught by Thich Nhat Hanh encourages meditators to visualize themselves as elements of nature:

> Breathing in, I know I am breathing in. Breathing out, I know I am breathing out.
> Breathing in, I see myself as a flower. Breathing out, I feel fresh.
> Breathing in, I see myself as a mountain. Breathing out, I feel solid.
> Breathing in, I see myself as still water. Breathing out, I reflect things as they are.
> Breathing in, I see myself as space. Breathing out, I feel free.

Although this exercise was originally presented as a meditation, not as a technique for enhancing sensitivity to the environment, it evokes ecologist

Aldo Leopold's 1949 warning that unless we learn to "think like a mountain," we will not be able to avoid ecological disaster.

Some practitioners use short verses (*gāthās*) as reminders of environmental awareness. Turning on a faucet, for example, they silently recite: "Water flows from the high mountains. / Water runs deep in the Earth. / Miraculously, water comes to us/and sustains all life." Robert Aitken, learning from the environment in the city, uses the occasion to make another vow:

> When I stroll around in the city
>   I vow with all beings
> to notice how lichen and grasses
> never give up in despair.

In Mahayana Buddhism, spiritual merit can be transferred to others, so some groups now end ceremonies with dedications to the well-being of the planet. At the Rochester Zen Center, participants chant: "Whatever merit comes to us from these offerings / We now return to the Earth, sea, and sky."

Cardinal Buddhist teachings invite fresh interpretations in environmental contexts. Consider ignorance, one of the "three poisons." The original meaning—that people are ignorant of their true nature and the true nature of existence—is as valid as ever. In addition, we seem to be increasingly ignorant of our place in nature. How many of us know where our water comes from, or where our garbage goes? How can we know what will become of nuclear waste twenty-five thousand years from now?

Likewise, the concept of impermanence is amplified today by the enormous loss of species. The notion of interdependence helps to shed light on the role of humans in the food chain. The doctrine of karma, if extended to the moral implications of actions affecting the environment, adds a Buddhist point of view to environmental ethics. A first law of eco-karma might be: what we do to the Earth, we do to ourselves. Are there meaningful ways to atone for the negative eco-karma that has already accumulated?

Several of these themes come to life in the work of Stephanie Kaza, who approaches environmental problems from a systems perspective. When a mixed cord of wood is delivered to her doorstep, she discovers that some of the wood is from distant sources, and realizes that the local supply of wood is being overharvested. Refilling the tank of her chain saw with a mix of gas and oil, Kaza continues to reflect:

> Gas and oil from where? The Persian Gulf, Alaska, off the coast of southern California? Through what war zones or ice floes has this gas traveled before entering the chain saw? How much has it already cost in transportation and energy to produce this liquid gold?. . . The chain saw brings us to the point of intimacy, the hinge point around which all aspects of the story turn—fire, woodpile, oil, mind, danger, connection—each interpenetrating in the meeting place of our bodies.

The woodpile that gets replenished is itself a system. In this way, commonplace tasks can direct attention to the ever-present web of mutual causality.

In a time of ecological crisis, to experience oneness with other beings and the Earth is also to feel pain. As Gary Snyder writes, "The extinction of a species, each one a pilgrim of four billion years of evolution, is an irreversible loss. The ending of the lines of so many creatures with whom we have traveled this far is an occasion for profound sorrow and grief." The balance between hope and despair is a delicate one. Buddhists in the past have succumbed to hopelessness especially when they feared that they were living in the last days of the Dharma. Most engaged Buddhists understand that too much despair vitiates the energy needed for constructive action. So does too much hope. Whether this is a time of perishing Dharma or flourishing Dharma, the plants must be watered.

According to traditional sources, Shakyamuni Buddha was assailed by severe torments before his breakthrough to enlightenment. When Mara, personification of all torments, challenged Shakyamuni's commitment as a seeker, Shakyamuni reached down with his right hand and lightly touched the Earth, because the Earth had intimately witnessed his long course of spiritual exertion. This Earth-touching posture became the classic visual representation of Shakyamuni's awakening. Self-realization, however transcendent, is also rooted in a place. Is being in touch with the Earth linked to enlightenment in ways that have not been fully examined? Could this distinctive image double as a symbol of profound spiritual *and* ecological awareness?

# Extending
## Compassionate Action

SAMANTABHADRA, one of the principal bodhisattvas in the Asian Buddhist pantheon, makes a stunning vow:

> May I purify oceans of lands, liberate oceans of beings, observe oceans of truths, plumb oceans of knowledge, perfect oceans of practices, fulfill oceans of vows, and serve oceans of Buddhas. As long as the Earth exists, as long as all beings exist, as long as acts and afflictions exist, so long will my vow remain.

Samantabhadra is traditionally depicted astride a majestic six-tusked white elephant, seated cross-legged on a luxuriant lotus saddle, hands held palm-to-palm at chest level. The bodhisattva's expression is always serene, but his elephant often seems to be grinning. Samantabhadra personifies "action conforming to reality or, broadly speaking, the active aspect of bodhisattvahood and Buddhahood." That is, he represents enlightened compassionate action.

Whereas the paths in the second ring of the Wheel highlight different *fields* of engagement (family, work, politics, environment), the paths in the outer ring highlight different *modes* of engagement. Here, the extension of compassionate action becomes a path in its own right. Whatever the state of one's engaged practice, it can almost always be extended—in scope, duration, skillfulness, depth of understanding, or degree of integration. Collective action directed toward structural change can be advanced by strengthening intentional communities, reinforcing links with like-minded groups, and reaching new audiences. Extension is also an abiding theme in Buddhism's historical and doctrinal development. When Shakyamuni created the Sangha, he boldly extended a welcome to members of all castes. In the "greater vehicle" of Mahayana Buddhism, the ability to achieve enlightenment is extended not only to laypeople, but ultimately to all existence—animal, mineral, or vegetable.

Activities that express this path vary greatly in outward form. When Patrick McMahon taught at an inner-city school in Berkeley, California, he sought to extend the domain of practice to his classroom:

> Unless I thought there was a point to Buddhist peacemakers working in the schools, reforming society from within, I wouldn't be there. . . . How do you teach peace in the war zone of present-day education? . . . How do you practice mindfulness, much less teach mindfulness, in the rat cage of an overcrowded classroom? How do you translate Buddhist teachings into the various languages of class, color, and culture of an inner-city school?

In Yonkers, New York, a Buddhist group under the leadership of Zen teacher Bernard Glassman set up housing for the homeless and created work programs, including a bakery, to employ the poor. When the socially progressive Zen bakery attracted a burst of publicity, it defined Zen "for hundreds of thousands of people who might never have heard of it before," according to Glassman. Once a year, in New York's Central Park, the Buddhist journal *Tricycle* sponsors "Change Your Mind Day." In a festive atmosphere, teachers from various lineages offer instruction in meditation to all who are interested, free of charge. That too is the spirit of this path. Change Your Mind Day participants have found that two thousand people meditating together in the heart of New York City create an exceptional quality of silence.

Most of us have areas in our lives that seem to fall outside our efforts to deepen awareness. It is possible, however, to notice those neglected places and consciously make them a part of practice. Jack Kornfield offers a meditation to advance the process:

> As you sense each area, hold it lightly in your heart and consider what it would mean to bring this too into your practice. Envision how your sense of the sacred could grow to include this in your practice with full attention and compassion, honoring these people, places, or activities. . . . Sense how each has a lesson to teach, how each area will bring a deepening of your attention and an opening of your compassion until nothing is excluded.

Although it lacks the thrust of a vow, this potentially unbounded practice emulates Samantabhadra's classic declaration.

There is a relationship between compassionate action, teaching, and other forms of expression. According to one sutra, a bodhisattva "knows exactly who is to be educated, how, and by what means, whether by the bodhisattva's teaching, physical appearance, practices, or bearing." Authentic teaching can take place in any walk of life (or path of the Wheel): to be a loving parent is a kind of teaching, to work harmoniously with others is a kind of teaching, to live in a balanced ecological relationship with one's surroundings is a kind of teaching, and so on. Robert Aitken asks, "How does my livelihood teach the Buddha's experience?" We often assume that insight is one thing, and the expression of insight is something else. However, the two—call them wisdom and compassion, or practice and engagement—are ultimately inseparable. This is a basic tenet of engaged Buddhism. Stephen Batchelor asserts:

> Awakening is only complete—in the same way that a work of art is only complete—when it finds an expression, a form, that translates one's experience in a way that makes it accessible to others. That again is the balance between wisdom and compassion. The creative process of expressing the Dharma is not just a question of

duplicating in words something etched somewhere in the privacy of my soul. The living process of understanding is formed through the encounter with another person, with the world.

Spiritually, transmission of the Dharma is a crucial, even a crowning form of expression. It too qualifies as compassionate action. Shakyamuni, teacher of teachers, once gazed out at the upturned faces of the disciples who had assembled for his lecture. Without a word, he took a flower and held it up. Only one of the monks, Mahakashyapa, smiled in comprehension. Then Shakyamuni announced to the assembly, "Mahakashyapa understands me completely. He is my spiritual heir." The image in the Wheel for this path alludes to that archetypal story, so rich in meaning. How does Shakyamuni, or anyone, communicate the inexpressible? And what realization enables Mahakashyapa, or anyone, to know that a single flower completely expounds the Dharma? The answer must be experienced, and confirmed.

Now that we have reached the outer ring of the Wheel, we are in a better position to note some of the ways in which the various paths relate to one another. For example, the present path forms a complementary pair with its visual opposite on the Wheel, the path of ease amid activity. Both are concerned with the integration of contemplation and action, but this one inclines toward action, and that one inclines toward contemplation. If I am using the Wheel as a guide to practice, I might choose to connect the path of compassionate action and the path of working with others—by committing myself more deeply to my job, or by finding new ways to serve others through my work. The present path also relates meaningfully to the path of moving into the world, depicted in the Wheel's hub. There one clarifies the intention to awaken and serve; here one checks to see how that initial resolve can be strengthened and amplified.

In other words, this mode is conducive to rebalancing and intensifying one's efforts. The practice of engaged Buddhism has its share of pitfalls.

Preoccupation with the ills of the world may cause one to lose sight of fundamental obstructions in one's own mind. Overattachment to good causes may stem from a sense of inner insufficiency. Doubts may arise about the validity of activities that bear little resemblance to traditional forms of practice. Or, satisfaction from the ability to incorporate diverse spheres into one's practice may lead to diminished vitality in seated meditation. Staying the course, and staying on course, are ever-present challenges. "We should have this compassion from the depths of our heart, as if it were nailed there," the Dalai Lama says. An old Zen capping phrase speaks of "a single iron rail extending ten thousand miles." The image is a metaphor for seamless Reality, but it also evokes the qualities that make bodhisattva practice strong: single-mindedness, staying in touch with one's deepest intentions, and perseverance over the long haul.

Samantabhadra's vehicle of choice is an elephant. The actual vehicles of compassionate action are beyond number. I offer a short verse for the road:

> magnificent Samantabhadra
> master of compassion in action
>
> treading the path
> steady
> as an elephant
>
> tender heart
> radiant
> as a lotus
>
> magnificent Samantabhadra
> our own deepest nature

# *Exploring New Terrain*

I N ITS LONG HISTORY, Buddhism has repeatedly adapted to different cultures and fresh circumstances. The lore of every major lineage honors pioneers and pilgrims who journeyed to new lands, semilegendary figures who still serve as archetypes of spiritually motivated exploration. The "first ancestor" of Zen, Bodhidharma, is said to have traveled all the way from India to China, reaching his goal by crossing the Yangtze River on a single reed. Padmasambhava trekked the Himalayas to bring Buddhism to Tibet. The Chinese master Chien-chen endured dangerous shipwrecks and other reversals to transmit a monastic lineage to Japan; by the time he arrived, he had gone blind. The first Westerners to seek Buddhism in once exotic places like Lhasa, Kandy, and Kyoto endured physical and emotional hardships in order to taste the wisdom of cultures that were profoundly foreign. The luminous courage of these pioneers is another attribute of bodhisattva mind.

What are the contours of *terra incognita* for engaged Buddhism today? Significant elements are new: methods of inner practice, forms of outer involvement, the ever-growing fields of application, even the forthright affirmation of engagement itself. As lines of inquiry go off in different directions, some quests bear fruit, and others do not. Individual and group explorations intertwine. Any map of the movement will accordingly have areas where only the coastlines can be sketched, like maps of the New World in the age of Magellan.

A Zen teacher has described Zen practice as "a lonely trek through winding canyons of shame and fear, across deserts of ecstatic visions and tormenting phantasms, around volcanoes of oozing ego, and through jungles of folly and delusion." Although those words point to an inner spiritual journey, they also apply to engagement in the world, where a sensitive person similarly struggles with shame, fear, folly, hopeful and bleak visions, and an ego that oozes forth incessantly. Meditators who assume that mindful participation in society is relatively well-marked territory are surprised to stumble into a samsaric wilderness not very far from the meditation room. New models are needed for personal transformation and for social transformation. "I don't think that we have too much sense of how to practice with a partner, a group, a community, or an ecosystem," says Donald Rothberg. Today, exploration may call for reinhabiting the land rather than leaving it, and crossing disciplinary boundaries rather than crossing oceans.

One contemporary exemplar of this path is the Dalai Lama. Since his daring flight from Tibet in 1959 (a literal crossing of unfamiliar terrain), he has become a world statesman and spiritual leader on a scale unprecedented in Buddhist history. In response to China's brutal occupation of Tibet, he has consistently embodied the Buddhist precept of nonviolence—a highly unconventional stance in the realm of realpolitik. His conviction that "violent oppressors are also worthy of compassion" challenges the gut reactions of Buddhists and non-Buddhists alike. Through his extensive travels and public appearances, he acquaints people with a Buddhist vision of a desirable society. In matters large and small, the Dalai Lama stirs controversy. When his face appeared on billboards and magazine back covers in an ad for Apple computers, the Tibetan cause may have been aided at the expense of Buddhism's critique of consumerism.

The greening of Buddhist communities illustrates innovative engagement on a group level. At the Green Gulch Zen Center, north of San Francisco, residents use water according to how much is actually available from local sources, thereby achieving water self-sufficiency. Other centers are experimenting with land stewardship, outdoor backpacking retreats, and ceremonies that acknowledge the presence of nonhuman neighbors. Will the successors to monasteries be "ecosteries"? A Samye Ling retreat center being built off the west coast of Scotland implements an energy-efficient design that will integrate water, crops, and waste.

In the spring of 1994, I took part in an unusual event at one of the most contaminated places on the planet. About sixty people gathered at the Nevada Nuclear Test Site, under the auspices of the Buddhist Peace Fellowship, to protest the nuclear explosions conducted at the site until recently; to grieve for the damage done to humans, wildlife, and the Earth; and to commemorate the Buddha's birthday on April 8. This was new terrain indeed, and our attempts to promote disarmament both outwardly and inwardly had an improvisational quality. At one point during walking meditation, the single-file line went right up to a barrier under the surveillance of five men in uniform. The barrier was actually a cattle guard, spaced iron bars at ground level. Anyone who stepped on it would be arrested. Around us, the wind kicked up dust (*radioactive* dust?), mocking all such boundaries. Hardly pausing, many walked silently across the barrier.

Opportunities for social action or service are often close at hand; big ideas and grand gestures are not required. Grassroots organizer Mirabai Bush offers five simple principles: be brave, start small, use what you've got, do something you enjoy, and don't overcommit. For example:

> This exercise may help you to find a means of service that will come from what you do well and love. Sit quietly. Either say out loud or write down the words, "The way I'd really love to help is. . . ." Keep it going. . . .

> One woman, troubled by the plight of homeless people in her area, wrote, "The way I'd really love to help is to work with homeless mothers, because I know if I were homeless I would be scared and tired. . . . What I'd really love to do is use my camera to take pictures, but what good would it do? What I'd really love to do is be together as people. . . ."

As the woman continued the exercise, ideas arose, and she was inspired to start a small project teaching homeless mothers how to photograph their children. The mothers developed a new sense of mastery, and their work led to a show that poignantly expressed their vision of the world.

The Wheel's image for this path portrays unexplored terrain. The bridge alludes to the creativity of engaged practice, its ability to connect homeless mothers and photography, or civil disobedience and Buddha's birthday. One of the abiding aims of Buddhism is to bridge the realm of awakening and the realm of suffering. A bridge is also a traditional reminder of spiritual purpose: "Upon seeing a bridge," one sutra states, "wish that all beings carry everyone across to liberation."

It is worthwhile at times simply to wander, as Taoist sages remind us. Byways reveal hidden vistas, and getting lost is a way of finding things. In one sense, we are always lost; in another sense, we are never lost. Gary Snyder offers a useful clarification when he notes that it is possible to be off the trail but still on the path:

> There is nothing like stepping away from the road and heading into a new part of the watershed. Not for the sake of newness, but for the sense of coming home to our whole terrain. "Off the trail" is another name for the Way, and sauntering off the trail is the practice of the wild. This is also where—paradoxically—we do our best work. But we need paths and trails and will always be maintaining them. You first must be on the path, before you can turn and walk into the wild.

John Seed reports an experience that seems to fit this off-the-trail, on-the-path model. Soon after he became deeply involved in the defense of rain forests, something unexpected happened:

> I stopped meditating. My practice just dropped away. I wasn't looking inside anymore. And I didn't have any particular explanation for this. I must say, at first it caused me quite a bit of anguish. . . . My sense is that I'm not getting lost from the path. This is what I'm meant to be doing. Perhaps one day that current will pick me up and I'll start meditating again. I haven't lost confidence in the practice. It's just that I was led somewhere else.

In spiritual training, as in most fields, there are learning curves and stages of apprenticeship, usually the longer the better. As Buddhist practice in the West continues to develop, individuals and groups are becoming increasingly skilled at finding their own way inwardly and outwardly. If the process remains on course, we learn how to learn, not only from teachers but also from ourselves. Eventually, we come to trust our own sense of direction. As rock climbers attest, there is almost always a route through new terrain, even up the face of the sheerest cliff. But we have to invent that route as we go.

The new century and millennium are another kind of unexplored terrain. Whatever the prospects of advancement, there will undoubtedly be fierce struggles over resources, ideologies, and ethnic loyalties. Will coming generations manage to weather the changes, the way Bodhidharma crossed the Yangtze, or will they be blinded by the upheavals, like shipwrecked Chien-chen? One thing is certain: bodhisattva courage will be required.

# At Ease Amid Activity

MAYLIE SCOTT, an ordained member of the Berkeley Zen Center, has been demonstrating for years against international arms traffic at the Concord Naval Weapons Station near Oakland, California. Sometimes she and fellow activists sit directly on the tracks used by supply trains bearing weapons. "I go out there and just take a deep breath," she reports. "It's partly the place, and partly the people who are so dedicated to freeing themselves and our society from our various addictions." She has found that it is possible to be at ease amid activity, and to remain calm under fire.

Buddhists aspire to remain composed in times of extremity. Whether a crisis is localized or widespread, a single clear-headed person can significantly affect others and the situation. Because the world is so often in dire straits, it is said that "all Buddhas sit in the middle of fire." During the Vietnam War, the monk Thich Quang Duc demonstrated this teaching in the most literal way possible, immolating himself on a Saigon street to call attention to the suffering in his country. A number of other Buddhist monks and nuns chose the same course. In light of such sacrifices, an ancient definition of a bodhisattva loses its rhetorical air: "Like a fire, a bodhisattva's mind constantly blazes up into good works for others. At the same time, he [or she] always remains merged in the calm of the trances and formless attainments."

Bodhisattvas are also in training to prepare for a future time of need. As the fires of greed and ignorance continue to rage across the landscape, many people and many other beings are already in crisis. A fifth of the world's population are desperately poor, and even in the United States a fifth of the children now live in poverty. Unimaginable calamities may lie ahead, whether caused by social, military, environmental, or other factors. Who will be ready when disaster strikes?

Meditation fosters the ability to remain centered amid ordinary activity and extreme conditions, so contemplation is integral to this path. In Buddhism, to be contemplative is not to be lost in thought. Far from being lax or passive, proper meditation requires active attention to experience, moment to moment. Meditation is itself an authentic response to suffering in the world. Engagement, when needed, calls for qualities that sitting practice cultivates, such as clarity, openness, and perseverance. Some Buddhist activists maintain that one cannot really change the world unless one sits. The challenge is not whether to meditate or be engaged, but how to meditate *and* be engaged. For Thich Nhat Hanh, "The question is how to engage without losing the contemplative life."

Basic guidelines for Buddhist-style meditation can be found in many sources. One contemporary teacher advises:

> Find a quiet, comfortable place. Sit still. Make sure the back is unsupported and upright, but not tense. Check to see if there are any points of tension in the body: the shoulders, the neck, around the eyes. Relax them. Take three long, slow, deep breaths. Then let the breathing resume its own rhythm, without interference or control.
>
> The formal practice of mindfulness begins with a heightened awareness of the sensory array that is the body. Central to this is breathing. When meditating on the breath, let go of any picture you have of some invisible stuff being sucked in then pumped out of the lungs. . . . Only when you start paying careful attention to

the breath do you notice how complex and subtle are the range of sensations involved. As each inhalation and exhalation take place, delve deeper into the multilayered intricacy of this vital act.

One might expect engaged Buddhists to take a dim view of monasticism and long retreats, which seem to point in an unworldly direction. Yet that is rarely the case. Robert Thurman, for example, supports monasticism and engagement with equal fervor:

> The most activist thing the peace movement, the engaged movement, in the West could do would be to crank up the generosity to provide a permanent free lunch to any group of people who want to take serious ordination, remembering that the key to monasticism is that you can be useless.

According to individual circumstances, most engaged Buddhists renew themselves periodically through contact with a spiritual teacher or attendance at retreats. Sulak Sivaraksa describes a typical regimen:

> Even those of us who are in society must return to these masters from time to time and look within. We must practice our meditation, our prayer, at least every morning or evening. . . . At least once a year we need to go to a retreat center to regain our spiritual strength, so we can return to confront society.

What appears to be withdrawal (or may indeed begin as withdrawal) can turn into something else. Michele McDonald-Smith, who leads Vipassana retreats, speaks from experience: "What's ironic to me is how much a deep sense of connection comes out of the profound solitude and silence of a retreat setting, how the ability to connect is related to the ability to have intimacy with oneself."

In the early stages of practice, one's state of mind in formal meditation and one's mind-state amid daily activities seem quite different. In time, attentiveness can be directed inwardly or outwardly with similar consistency. Even when moving about, it becomes possible to apply the ideal of voluntary simplicity to awareness in the present moment—by not allowing the mind to be distracted by this or that. For beginners and veterans alike, a fundamental technique is to take a few mindful breaths. Catch your breath. A moment of mindfulness can become a moment of calm; a moment of calm can become a moment of mindfulness. In my car, if I am paying attention, I use red lights as reminders to take a breath and take a breather.

Years ago, I spent a morning moving heavy boulders under the supervision of the late Zen teacher Shunryu Suzuki, who was building a garden at Tassajara, near Carmel, California. Just as all of us in the work crew were getting completely caught up in the task, certain that we were impressing the teacher with our diligence, he said softly, "Let's have some tea."

Ideally, action embodies the fruits of contemplation, though this kind of action is difficult to describe. Taoists use the tantalizing term *wu-wei*, for which no English translation ever seems adequate. "Non-purposive doing" is one approximation. A kindred notion is action from a nonaction base. When there is effort, it is supposed to have an effortless quality, like rowing a boat gently down a stream. On this path, an adept also knows how to *dis*engage without being irresponsible. Sometimes the best possible course is to do nothing. Don't just *do* something—*sit* there! In the realm of expression, this path suggests an economical use of words, and an appreciation of judicious silence. A monk once pointed to these qualities when he praised his former master: "My teacher was great in what he said, but he was even greater in what he didn't say."

Buddhism has a rich store of portraits of equanimity, from Shakyamuni in meditation to Feng-kan sleeping beside a tiger. One of the best known images is the bodhisattva Kuan-yin in a pose of "royal ease." In this posture, Kuan-yin sits on a dais, facing forward. One leg touches the ground, but the other rests comfortably on the dais, bent knee raised. Kuan-yin's arm is lightly draped over her raised knee. The figure is centered, still, and alert, poised at a point of balance between an inner focus and an outer focus. Hakuin, the versatile Japanese Zen master, liked to paint pictures of Kuan-yin sitting gracefully in this fashion. In traditional Zen, it was considered bad form to praise someone directly, and good form to laud by "slander," so when Hakuin wanted to extol Kuan-yin verbally, he had to honor this code. On one of his paintings, he wrote, "She enjoys her spare moments when there is no connection with human beings. Who says her vow to awaken sentient beings is deep?"

While Hakuin's comment represents Zen-style praise, it also hints at another theme: the affinity between the allure of profound contemplation and the allure of withdrawal. Many engaged Buddhists treat the potential link between meditation and withdrawal as a latent but resolvable tension. In the original Wheel of Life, the highest aim was to get off the Wheel entirely, to become free of the samsaric cycle of birth and death. Of the ten paths in the Wheel of Engaged Buddhism, the present path comes closest to offering a way out. It sits at the bottom of the Wheel, the resting point of a pendulum, the place where a ferris wheel stops. However, in this Wheel, as in Mahayana Buddhism generally, there is no rush for the exits. Joanna Macy explains why: "How can I get off the wheel? I am the wheel."

# Spreading Joy
## in Ten Directions

T HE LEFT SIDE of the Wheel illustrates the path of joyous participation in the world. From the seeds of compassion come the flowers of awareness and the fruits of engagement. "Ten directions" refers to the eight cardinal compass points, plus up and down. In other words, when someone can act in an unhindered manner on behalf of others, handling inner and outer work gladly, the path is open in all directions. "When I live committed like this, my life is full of joy," declares John Seed.

Engaged Buddhists are demonstrating the spirit of this path in personal, social, and global arenas, and in ways that transcend those distinctions. In the winter of 1993, as war raged in the former Yugoslavia, Fran Peavey was deeply disturbed by the atrocities committed against women. She decided to go to the war-torn country and offer whatever assistance she could, but she did not want to arrive empty-handed. Then she had an idea:

> In one of my morning meditations, the idea came to me of making small bundles of sweet-smelling soaps, shampoos, make-up, and scarves for the women in the former Yugoslavia who had been raped or lost their homes. Maybe it could help them remember some of the wonderful things about being a woman that a rape tends to erase. Maybe they could feel the connection of women

from other parts of the world who sent those packages. I don't know where that idea came from, because I never use make-up or some of the other items I imagined for those bundles.

In the face of real atrocities, would such a gesture be meaningful? Do "random kindness and senseless acts of beauty" have a place alongside the responses of governments and large organizations? Peavey herself had doubts. She contacted some Yugoslav women and made other inquiries. Eventually, after months of preparation, she and a partner hand-delivered eight thousand gift packages, individually wrapped by women in America and Australia, to victims of the war. When Peavey saw the Yugoslav women receive their packages, her lingering doubts dissolved. "Later, when some of them invited us into their rooms, they might be wearing a new scarf or perfume, and we could see that they were happy." After returning home, she organized further relief efforts, sending medical supplies and helping the women find markets for embroidered bracelets. For Peavey, the gift project became a way to "build bridges and open hearts in a situation full of fear, suspicion, and hatred."

Generosity is a primary virtue in Buddhism. In the past, some teachers have attached greater importance to giving than to meditation or wisdom. According to a traditional classification, there is tentative giving, friendly giving, and princely giving. When one happily shares or gives up the best one has, whether it be time, energy, or material resources, that is princely giving. Josh Schrei, who works with the Free Tibet movement, is a member of the first generation to grow up in an American Buddhist community (his parents were residents of the Zen Center of Rochester, New York). Recently, Schrei made the following observation about his upbringing: "One of the things that I took on as a child at the Zen Center was that selfless giving is basically the highest human ideal, that I should always think of others, that I should be ready to give myself up for others."

A simple exercise fosters generosity: Undertake to act on every generous thought that comes to mind, even if the next thought offers a plausible reason not to act so charitably. (Some common-sense limits are acceptable.) Attempting to uphold this guideline, you may notice how often you censor your own generous impulses.

What is called "helping" is usually much more. We engage not only to address a problem, but also to connect with others, to confirm our own humanity, and to acknowledge the mysterious web of interdependence. In the process, something happens to the supposed boundary between the helper and the helped: its insubstantiality is revealed, or it dissolves altogether. Traditional descriptions of the "perfection of giving" point to this experience of oneness, though today the language sounds arcane:

> Here a bodhisattva gives a gift, and he does not apprehend a self, nor a recipient, nor a gift; also no reward of his giving. He surrenders that gift to all beings, but he apprehends neither beings nor self. He dedicates that gift to supreme enlightenment, but he does not apprehend any enlightenment.

Thich Nhat Hanh says that he experiences something comparable when he translates orphans' applications for sponsorship. Before he reads anything in the file, he looks closely at a photograph of the orphan, studying the child's expression and features. Then:

> I feel a deep link between myself and each child, which allows me to enter a special communion with them. . . . I no longer see an "I" who translates the sheets to help each child, I no longer see a child who received love and help. The child and I are one: no one pities; no one asks for help; no one helps. There is no task, no social work to be done, no compassion, no special wisdom.

In such moments of nondiscrimination, contemplative practice and social engagement converge seamlessly.

Spiritually mature people radiate a rare quality of freedom. They act with a kind of inner and outer spaciousness that is felt and shared by others present. This has nothing to do with the common misconception that freedom lies in following impulses at will. (A recent ad for cell phones proclaims, "I'm free to do what I want any old time. Let freedom ring!") When Westerners began to practice Buddhism, some equated liberation with full satori, while others assumed that an enlightened person was free to act any way he or she chose, exempt from karmic repercussions. However, on the path of spreading joy, freedom can be experienced in every moment, amid the usual duties and constraints, whether one is taking a shower or talking with the boss.

Today, an increasing number of people have access to the Buddhist understanding of spiritual freedom, as expressed in enlightenment, and the Western ideal of political freedom, as expressed in democracy. For the first time, it may be possible to realize these two dimensions in concert, pursuing a path of emancipation both in one's personal life and in the healing of this world. And that, after all, is the creed of a bodhisattva: one can attain true liberation only through helping others become liberated. No one is free until everyone is free.

Genuine humility and openness, the qualities of a beginner's mind, are especially important *after* one has made some progress on a spiritual path. In some streams of Buddhism, such as Zen, a highly developed person has no obvious signs of special attainment. If such a person were riding on a bus with you, you might not notice her. In place of the supernormal powers sometimes ascribed to an enlightened Buddha, Zen substitutes pure, spontaneous participation in the world. "My master can walk on water," boasts a monk in a well-known anecdote. "Well, my master's powers are even greater than that," replies a second monk. "When he's hungry, he eats. When he's tired, he sleeps." That understanding returns us to daily life in the world as it is, the true place of practice.

The theme of ordinariness applies equally to the realm of engagement. With or without great leaders, it is ordinary people who bravely and unselfishly change the world for the better. In many cases, the actions that must be taken to respond to the cries of the world are simple steps rather than extraordinary measures. If engaged Buddhism continues to develop along current lines, Buddhism's center of gravity will shift away from institutions toward the actual experience of engaged practitioners, working together.

Viewed as part of a sequence, the path of spreading joy in ten directions represents a culmination. Whereas the initial steps of moving into the world may have been tentative, now one goes forward briskly, with assurance and gratitude. Viewed independently of a sequence, this path is equal to each of the other paths. Since joy is realized in daily life, the family, the workplace, politics, and so on, a second implication of "ten directions" is all ten paths on the Wheel. "There is no way to happiness; happiness is the way."

A lotus bud is perfectly a bud just as it is, without having to become a seed-bearing flower. An acorn is perfectly an acorn just as it is, without having to become an oak tree. In that sense, any point on a spiritual path is a point of completion. At the same time, a spiritual path is endless. One of the meanings of being on a path is that we have yet to arrive. There will always be more to see, feel, learn, and communicate. There will always be new obstacles to surmount, more ways to help, and deeper awakenings. Flowers everywhere!

# N

AN-YÜEH, a Ch'an (Zen) master of eighth-century China, once came upon a student meditating earnestly. Without a word, the master picked up a tile that happened to be lying nearby and began to rub it vigorously. The student's concentration was broken. He looked up and asked, "Master, what are you doing?" Nan-yüeh replied, "I'm making a mirror." "But," the student protested, "you can't make a mirror by polishing a tile!" "That's right," said the master. "And you can't make a Buddha by sitting in meditation."

What was Nan-yüeh teaching? It is unlikely that he was telling the student that meditation is pointless. Perhaps he was intimating some central tenets of Zen practice—everyone is inherently a Buddha from the beginning; enlightenment is not a matter of getting something one lacks; and proper meditation reflects that understanding. The act of rubbing the tile would then double as a concrete expression of Buddha nature, which is not confined to a seated posture or any other fixed form.

Good Zen anecdotes almost always yield more than one meaning. In this case, Nan-yüeh's cryptic demonstration may also imply that meditation practice, by itself, cannot bring anyone to full spiritual maturity, or Buddhahood. There must also be bodhisattva practice, which is expressed in an infinite variety of ways. So suggested Tsung-mi, an influential master who lived a century after Nan-yüeh. Wisdom and compassion must be *enacted*. Read in this way, the story also illustrates a cardinal principle of engaged Buddhism.

The ten paths pictured in the Wheel testify to the diversity and adaptability of contemporary bodhisattva practice. Although meditation may be indispensable, neither it nor any other single discipline can stand (or sit) alone. Engaged practice also entails development of character, cultivation of generosity and other virtues, refinement of ethical sensitivity, and the day-by-day activation of compassion. The continuous process of reshaping practice is itself an essential part of practice. It is not a matter of finding a specific technique or formula and then repeating it mechanically. That would be like rubbing a tile to make a mirror.

The Japanese lay Zen teacher Hisamatsu Shin'ichi (1889–1980) believed that a spiritually authentic life in the modern world rests on three components: penetrating investigation of the self, penetrating investigation of the world, and penetrating investigation of history. On a personal level, these disciplines are none other than practice, engagement, and study. (Here, "practice" refers to traditional spiritual training, and "study" is not confined to the academy.) Ideally, those three elements complement and reinforce one another, like the legs of a tripod.

The same goes for engaged Buddhism as a movement. Its potential will be fulfilled through continued development in three domains that fit this model: practices that enhance inner and outer awareness, modes of effective involvement in the world (including the environment), and incisive analysis of social conditions and social change. The exploration of bodhisattva mind is a telling investigation of the self. Aung San Suu Kyi's nonviolent fight for democracy, Issan Dorsey's humane hospice work, and all of the more common forms of commitment pertain to investigation of the world. The effort to understand the implications of engaged Buddhism in light of Buddhist tradition is a relevant variant of historical investigation.

Imagine a mountain with several trails to the top. From the base of each trail, the view is limited and one-sided. In a similar way, any of the ten paths in the Wheel, or any of Hisamatsu's three arenas of inquiry, have a partial quality. Closer to the peak, the trails begin to converge, the view expands, and the scenes from the different paths increasingly overlap. That corresponds to integration of the various elements that make up an aware, committed life. At the summit, the trails meet, and the view is unimpeded. The panorama is the same no matter which trail one hiked to get there: a radiant mandala of bodhisattva mind, all the way to the horizon.

# Notes

INTRODUCTION

8. *One elaborate blueprint* See Collett Cox, "Attainment through Abandonment: The Sarvāstivādin Path of Removing Defilements," in Robert E. Buswell, Jr., and Robert M. Gimello, eds., *Paths to Liberation: The Mārga and Its Transformations in Buddhist Thought* (Honolulu: University of Hawaii Press, 1992), 63.

8. *The Sanskrit word for spiritual path* This list of mārga meanings is abridged from Jeffrey Hopkins, "A Tibetan Perspective on the Nature of the Spiritual Experience," in Buswell and Gimello, *Paths to Liberation*, 247.

9. *attainment of full Buddhahood would require* This calculation is found in Donald S. Lopez, Jr., "Paths Terminable and Interminable," in Buswell and Gimello, *Paths to Liberation*, 147.

9. *Some recent coinages are thought-provoking* Stephen Batchelor discusses "a culture of awakening" in *Buddhism Without Beliefs* (New York: Riverhead Books, 1997), 109 and passim. Robert Thurman contemplates a "politics of enlightenment" in *Inner Revolution: Life, Liberty, and the Pursuit of Real Happiness* (New York: Riverhead Books, 1998), vii and passim. Chögyam Trungpa writes about "an enlightened society" in *Shambhala: The Sacred Path of the Warrior* (Boulder: Shambhala, 1984), 25 and passim. Stephanie Kaza speaks of "ecological awakening" in "Making a Marriage with the Earth," in *Turning Wheel: Journal of the Buddhist Peace Fellowship* (fall 1991), 15. I propose the term "eco-karma" in Kenneth Kraft, "Nuclear Ecology and Engaged Buddhism," in Mary Evelyn Tucker and Duncan Ryūken Williams, eds., *Buddhism and Ecology: The Interconnection of Dharma and Deeds* (Cambridge: Harvard University Press, 1997), 277–78.

10. *Robert Aitken, in a recent book* See *The Dragon Who Never Sleeps: Verses for Zen Buddhist Practice* (Berkeley: Parallax Press, 1992).

10. *We are learning how necessary personal development is* "Letters," in *Turning Wheel* (summer 1997), 5.

11. *Social action is itself a kind of meditation* Philip Kapleau, *Awakening to Zen* (New York: Scribner, 1997), 96.

11. *the 'unit' of enlightenment is not the single person* Jeanne Achterberg and Donald Rothberg, "Relationship as Spiritual Practice," in *ReVision* 19:2 (fall 1996), 3.

11. *This is a step beyond the monastery walls* Robert Aitken, "Precepts and Responsible Practice," in Arnold Kotler, ed., *Engaged Buddhist Reader* (Berkeley: Parallax Press, 1996), 237.

11. *Shakyamuni envisioned the first such image* The Dalai Lama summarizes the traditional account of the first painting of the Wheel of Life in *The Meaning of Life from a Buddhist Perspective* (Boston: Wisdom Publications, 1992), 12–13.

12. *The Dharma has no speech* The quotation by Kūkai is from Ryusaku Tsunoda, Wm. Theodore de Bary, and Donald Keene, eds., *Sources of Japanese Tradition*, vol. 1 (New York: Columbia University Press, 1969), 137–38 (slightly edited).

12. *The Wheel of Life is known throughout Asia* For a good image of the Wheel of Life, see Dalai Lama, *The Meaning of Life from a Buddhist Perspective*, 12–13.

12. *An East Asian variant of the Wheel of Life* For an image of this variant, see W. Zwalf, ed., *Buddhism: Art and Faith* (London: British Museum Publications, 1985), 275. The four paths of release are those of the arhat, pratyekabuddha, bodhisattva, and buddha.

12. *the Ten Oxherding Pictures* An accessible source is Philip Kapleau, *The Three Pillars of Zen*, rev. ed. (New York: Doubleday, 1989), 313–25.

13. *the meditative Path of Calm* For the image and a commentary, see Kalu Rinpoche, *Luminous Mind: The Way of the Buddha* (Boston: Wisdom Publications, 1997), 155–58.

13. *probably have historical links* See Jan Fontein and Money L. Hickman, *Zen Painting and Calligraphy* (Boston: Museum of Fine Arts, 1970), 113.

13. *Maybe today's socially engaged Buddhists* Kenneth Kraft, "Practicing Peace: Social Engagement in Western Buddhism," in *Journal of Buddhist Ethics* 2 (1995); http://jbe.la.psu.edu.

14. *Avalokiteshvara (Chinese: Kuan-yin)* Whenever possible, I will refer to bodhisattvas by the name that is most familiar to Westerners, even though this principle does not permit linguistic/cultural consistency.

14. *the path for a bodhisattva-in-training classically has ten stages* See Robert E. Buswell, Jr. and Robert M. Gimello, "Introduction," in Buswell and Gimello, *Paths to Liberation*, 8.

15. *The object of gaining an insight* Kapleau, *Awakening to Zen*, 96.

15. *the "most underrated idea"* Janny Scott, "In Praise of Uncertainty and Other Underappreciated Concepts," *New York Times,* January 10, 1998. K. Anthony Appiah of Harvard was the scholar who chose kindness.

15. *My religion is kindness.* Cited in Jon Kabat-Zinn, *Wherever You Go, There You Are: Mindfulness Meditation in Everyday Life* (New York: Hyperion, 1994), 168.

## Navigating the Wheel

17. *The turning wheel is a powerful symbol*   Joanna Macy, *World As Lover, World As Self* (Berkeley: Parallax Press, 1991), 238.

19. *A flower is always receiving non-flower elements*   Thich Nhat Hanh, *Breathe! You Are Alive: Sutra on the Full Awareness of Breathing,* rev. ed. (Berkeley: Parallax Press, 1996), 67–68.

22. *To glimpse one's own true nature*   Peter Matthiessen, *The Snow Leopard* (New York: Viking, 1978), 232–33.


## Moving into the World

26. *It was a picture*   Vanya Palmers, "What Can I Do?" in *Turning Wheel* (winter 1993), 15.

26. *Somehow I found myself involved*   Wes Nisker, "The Rain Forest as Teacher: An Interview with John Seed," in *Inquiring Mind* 8:2 (spring 1992), 1.

26. *The root of all Buddhist teaching is compassion*   Dalai Lama, *The Meaning of Life from a Buddhist Perspective,* 4–5.

26. *A beginner bodhisattva*   Robert A. F. Thurman, trans., *The Tibetan Book of the Dead* (New York: Bantam Books, 1994), 247.

27. *What are the roots of my own caring action?*   These questions are raised (in a slightly different order) by Ram Dass and Mirabai Bush in *Compassion in Action: Setting Out on the Path of Service* (New York: Bell Tower, 1992), xii, 12.

27. *Choose a nice road for your practice*   Thich Nhat Hanh, *A Guide to Walking Meditation* (Nyack, NY: Fellowship of Reconciliation, 1985), 13.

28. *You can gradually begin to include others*   This quotation and more detailed instructions are found in Jack Kornfield, *A Path with Heart: A Guide through the Perils and Promises of Spiritual Life* (New York: Bantam Books, 1993), 20.

28. *Waking up in the morning*   Aitken, *The Dragon Who Never Sleeps,* 3.

28. *For the past fifteen years*   Barbara Gates and Wes Nisker, "Thinking Like Water: An Interview with Tova Green and Fran Peavey," in *Inquiring Mind* 12:2 (spring 1996), 7.

29. *There are so many urgent problems*   Thich Nhat Hanh, *Love in Action: Writings on Nonviolent Social Change* (Berkeley: Parallax Press, 1993), 136.

29. *We can, of course, help through all that we* do   Ram Dass and Paul Gorman, *How Can I Help?* (New York: Alfred A. Knopf, 1985), 227.

29. *Practice is bodhisattvic*   Victoria Kieburtz, "Trekking the Six Realms," in *Zen Bow* 20:2 (spring 1998), 13.


## Cultivating Awareness in Daily Life

31. *Those who see worldly life as an obstacle*   Cited in Claude Whitmyer, ed., *Mindfulness and Meaningful Work: Explorations in Right Livelihood* (Berkeley: Parallax Press, 1994), 21.

31. *Several recent books*   See Charlotte Joko Beck, *Everyday Zen: Love and Work* (New

York: HarperCollins, 1989); Pema Chodron, *Start Where You Are* (New York: Random House, 1994); Jon Kabat-Zinn, *Wherever You Go, There You Are: Mindfulness Meditation in Everyday Life* (New York: Hyperion, 1994); Thich Nhat Hanh, *Peace Is Every Step: The Path of Mindfulness in Everyday Life* (New York: Bantam, 1991); Thich Nhat Hanh, *Present Moment, Wonderful Moment: Mindfulness Verses for Daily Living* (Berkeley: Parallax Press, 1990); and Pabongka Rinpoche, *Liberation in the Palm of Your Hand* (Boston: Wisdom Publications, 1997).

32. *One day a man of the people said to Zen master Ikkyū*  Cited in Kapleau, *The Three Pillars of Zen*, 10–11.

33. *Fleas, lice*  Daisetz T. Suzuki, *Zen and Japanese Culture* (Princeton: Princeton University Press, 1973), 237.

33. *When I get depressed, off course*  Rebecca Capolungo-Hartman, posted on the Internet, February 2, 1998.

34. *calls these precepts "mindfulness trainings"*  See Thich Nhat Hanh, *For a Future to Be Possible: Commentaries on the Five Wonderful Precepts* (Berkeley: Parallax Press, 1993), 3-79.

34. *pick a precept*  See Jack Kornfield, *A Path with Heart: A Guide through the Perils and Promises of Spiritual Life* (New York: Bantam Books,1993), 304–5.

35. *the global marketing of Coca-cola*  See Juliet B. Schor, *The Overspent American: Upscaling, Downshifting, and the New Consumer* (New York: Basic Books, 1998), 90.

35. *The forests! The forests!*  Stephanie Kaza, *The Attentive Heart: Conversations with Trees* (New York: Ballantine Books, 1993), 161–62.

EMBRACING FAMILY

41. *With my own "suffering" diminished*  Victoria Kieburtz, "Trekking the Six Realms," 14.

41. *hard to get the children herded into the car pool*  Gary Snyder, *The Practice of the Wild* (San Francisco: North Point Press, 1990), 153.

41. *Part of your work as a parent is to keep growing*  Myla and Jon Kabat-Zinn, *Everyday Blessings: The Inner Work of Mindful Parenting* (New York: Hyperion, 1997), 387.

41. *Try seeing the children as your teachers*  Kabat-Zinn, *Wherever You Go, There You Are*, 256.

41. *Instead of sitting up all night in mediation*  Jack Kornfield, "Respect for Parenting, Respect for Children," in *Inquiring Mind* 8:2 (spring 1992), 9.

41. *It lives on the altar in Jason's room*  Lee Klinger-Lesser, "Karma, Dharma, and Diapers," in Sandy Eastoak, ed., *Dharma Family Treasures: Sharing Mindfulness with Children* (Berkeley: North Atlantic Books, 1994), 67.

42. *It awakens my brain*  Ari Gervon-Kessler, "How I Meditate," in Eastoak, *Dharma Family Treasures*, 183.

42. *Mom, how do you fix the precepts*  Julie Quinn, "Falling Off the Precepts," in Eastoak, *Dharma Family Treasures*, 198.

42. *Innumerable labors did not bring us this food*   Dhyana Cabarga, "'Not' Chanting," in Eastoak, *Dharma Family Treasures*, 124–25.

42. *If you cannot serve your wife or husband*   Thich Nhat Hanh, *The Miracle of Mindfulness: A Manual on Meditation*, rev. ed. (Boston: Beacon Press, 1987), 75.

43. *If your friends and students are dying*   David Schneider, *Street Zen: The Life and Work of Issan Dorsey* (Boston: Shambhala, 1993), 173 (Schneider's recollection of a Dorsey statement).

## Working with Others

45. *The Buddha, in his wisdom, made 'right livelihood'*   Cited in Rick Fields et al., *Chop Wood, Carry Water: A Guide to Finding Spiritual Fulfillment in Everyday Life* (New York: Tarcher/Putnam, 1984), 110–11.

46. *Are certain jobs simply immoral?*   Some of these questions are adapted from Toni Packer, "What is Right Livelihood?" in Whitmyer, *Mindfulness and Meaningful Work*, 57–58.

47. *Would you be willing to be less efficient?*   Sam Keen, "Work and Worth: The High Price of Success," in Whitmyer, *Mindfulness and Meaningful Work*, 202.

47. *pulled out a package of the little green dots*   Saki F. Santorelli, "Mindfulness and Mastery," in Whitmyer, *Mindfulness and Meaningful Work*, 233.

48. *Aware of the suffering caused by unmindful speech*   Thich Nhat Hanh, *For a Future To Be Possible*, 4.

48. *moneytheism*   See David R. Loy, "The Religion of the Market," in *Journal of the American Academy of Religion* 65:2 (summer 1997), 275–90.

48. *Is business compatible with practice?*   Barry Keesan, "Living on the Edge," in *Zen Bow* 16:3 (summer 1994), 15.

48. *There is enough for everyone's need*   Cited in Joanna Macy, "Sarvodaya Means Everybody Wakes Up," in Whitmyer, *Mindfulness and Meaningful Work*, 163.

48. *A limousine is not an acquired taste*   Cited in Jonathan Schell, "The Post-Monica Era," in *The Nation* (April 27, 1998), 7.

49. *business is destroying the world*   Paul Hawken, *The Ecology of Commerce: A Declaration of Sustainability* (New York: HarperCollins, 1993), 3.

49. *in the midst of our muddy capitalist swamp*   Keesan, "Living on the Edge," 17.

50. *We work hard because there is someone*   Norman Fischer, "On Zen Work," in *Turning Wheel* (winter 1997), 15.

## Participating in Politics

51. *if you're meditating and a mosquito comes*   Claudia Dreifus, "The Passion of Suu Kyi," in *New York Times Magazine* (January 7, 1996), 36.

52. *Engaged Buddhism holds that inner peace*   See Kenneth Kraft, ed., *Inner Peace, World Peace: Essays on Buddhism and Nonviolence* (Albany: State University of New York Press, 1992).

52. *Buddhist Peace Fellowship*   Buddhist Peace Fellowship, P.O. Box 4650, Berkeley, CA

94704; 510/655-6169; www.bpf.org/bpf. Also see Kenneth Kraft, "Prospects of a Socially Engaged Buddhism," in Kraft, *Inner Peace, World Peace*, 23–28.

52. *International Network of Engaged Buddhists* International Network of Engaged Buddhists, P.O. Box 19, Mahadthai Post Office, Bangkok 10206, Thailand; tel/fax [662-] 433-7169; ineb@loxinfo.co.th.

53. *diet for a mindful society* Thich Nhat Hanh, *For a Future to be Possible*, 62–79.

53. *Consumer culture works hand-in-glove with greed* Sulak Sivaraksa, "Buddhism and Contemporary International Trends," in Kraft, *Inner Peace, World Peace*, 132.

53 *dhammic socialism* See Donald K. Swearer, ed., *Me and Mine: Selected Essays of Bhikkhu Buddhadāsa* (Albany: State University of New York Press, 1989).

53. *zone of peace* Sidney Piburn, ed., *The Nobel Peace Prize and the Dalai Lama* (Ithaca: Snow Lion, 1990), 40–45.

54. *antisocial hang-up* Ken Jones, *Beyond Optimism: A Buddhist Political Ecology* (Oxford: Jon Carpenter Publishing, 1993), 163.

54. *Today, a bodhisattva should be a politician* Nanao Sakaki, "Nanao Sakaki: Poet, Wanderer, Naturalist," in *Shambhala Sun* 4:2 (November 1995), 47.

54. *Efforts to bring awareness and wisdom* Donald Rothberg, "Responding to the Cries of the World: Socially Engaged Buddhism in North America," in Charles S. Prebish and Kenneth K. Tanaka, eds., *Faces of Buddhism in America* (Berkeley: University of California Press, 1998), 274.

54. *have to be working for peace* Thich Nhat Hanh, *Being Peace* (Berkeley: Parallax Press, 1987), 98.

55. *I feel a tension between creating programs* Tova Green, "Working for Peace and Justice in Cambridge: A Profile of Cathy Hoffman," in *Turning Wheel*, (fall 1997), 18.

55. *Find ways to be with those who are suffering* Thich Nhat Hanh, *Interbeing: Fourteen Guidelines for Engaged Buddhism*, rev. ed. (Berkeley: Parallax Press, 1993), 17.

55. *In the moment you feel compassion* Sogyal Rinpoche, *The Tibetan Book of Living and Dying* (New York: HarperCollins, 1993), 199. See also Joanna Macy, "Taking Heart: Spiritual Exercises for Social Activists," in Fred Eppsteiner, ed., *The Path of Compassion: Writings on Socially Engaged Budhism* (Berkeley: Parallax Press, 1988), 205–7.

56. *Often I feel discouraged* Alan Senauke, "Coordinator's Report," in *Turning Wheel* (spring 1993), 44.

CARING FOR THE EARTH

59. *The path of caring for the Earth draws upon the resources* See Stephanie Kaza and Kenneth Kraft, eds., *Dharma Rain: Sources of Buddhist Environmentalism* (Boston: Shambhala, forthcoming 1999).

60. *a greening of the self* See Joanna Macy, "The Greening of the Self," in Allan Hunt Badiner, ed., *Dharma Gaia: A Harvest of Essays in Buddhism and Ecology* (Berkeley: Parallax Press, 1990), 53–63.

60. *I'm going to practice in the trees*   Ecosattva, "Universal Chainsaw, Universal Forest," in *Turning Wheel* (winter 1998), 33.

61. *nuclear guardianship*   Joanna Macy, *World As Lover, World As Self*, 220–25, 234–37.

61. *I think I developed some qualities in meditation*   Nisker, "The Rain Forest as Teacher," 6.

61. *Breathing in, I know I am breathing in*   Thich Nhat Hanh, *Touching Peace: Practicing the Art of Mindful Living* (Berkeley: Parallax Press, 1992), 11–12.

62. *think like a mountain*   Aldo Leopold, *A Sand County Almanac* (Oxford: Oxford University Press, 1949, 1968), 129–37.

62. *Water flows from the high mountains*   Thich Nhat Hanh, *Present Moment, Wonderful Moment*, 9.

62. *When I stroll around in the city*   Aitken, *The Dragon Who Never Sleeps*, 42.

62. *Whatever merit comes to us*   Kenneth Kraft, "The Greening of Buddhist Practice," in Roger S. Gottlieb, ed., *This Sacred Earth: Religion, Nature, Environment* (New York: Routledge, 1996), 487.

63. *Gas and oil from where?*   Kaza, *The Attentive Heart*, 167–172.

63. *The extinction of a species*   Snyder, *The Practice of the Wild*, 176.


EXTENDING COMPASSIONATE ACTION

67. *May I purify oceans of lands*   Thomas Cleary, trans., *The Flower Ornament Scripture* (Boston: Shambhala, 1993), 1514–16. I have excerpted passages from a longer vow, originally in verse.

67. *action conforming to reality*   Thomas Cleary, *Entry Into the Inconceivable: An Introduction to Hua-yen Buddhism* (Honolulu: University of Hawaii Press, 1983), 201.

68. *Buddhist peacemakers working in the schools*   Patrick McMahon, "The Practice of Education," in *Turning Wheel* (summer 1991), 14.

68. *for hundreds of thousands of people*   Bernard Glassman and Rick Fields, *Instructions to the Cook: A Zen Master's Lessons for Living A Life That Matters* (New York: Bell Tower, 1996), x.

69. *As you sense each area*   Kornfield, *A Path with Heart*, 197.

69. *knows exactly who is to be educated*   *Ratnagotravibhāga* I, in Edward Conze et al., eds., *Buddhist Texts Through the Ages* (New York: Harper & Row, 1964), 130 (edited slightly).

69. *How does my livelihood teach*   Robert Aitken, *Encouraging Words: Zen Buddhist Teachings for Western Students* (New York: Pantheon Books, 1993), 111.

69. *Awakening is only complete*   Stephen Batchelor, "The Agnostic Buddhist," in *Zen Bow* 18:4 (fall 1996), 15.

70. *he took a flower and held it up*   See Katsuki Sekida, *Two Zen Classics* (New York: Weatherhill, 1977), 41.

71. *We should have this compassion from the depths of our hearts*   Cited in Paul Williams, *Mahāyāna Buddhism: The Doctrinal Foundations* (London: Routledge, 1989), 199.

EXPLORING NEW TERRAIN

74. *a lonely trek through winding canyons*   Philip Kapleau, "The Private Encounter with the Master," in Kenneth Kraft, ed., *Zen: Tradition and Transition* (New York: Grove Press, 1988), 47.

74. *how to practice with a partner, a group*   Donald Rothberg, "How Straight Is the Spiritual Path? Conversations with Buddhist Teachers Joseph Goldstein, Jack Kornfield, and Michele McDonald-Smith," in *ReVision* 19:1 (summer 1996), 38.

74. *violent oppressors are also worthy*   Robert A. F. Thurman, "Tibet and the Monastic Army of Peace," in Kraft, *Inner Peace, World Peace*, 87.

75. *The greening of Buddhist communities*   See Stephanie Kaza, "American Buddhist Responses to the Land: Ecological Practice at Two West Coast Retreat Centers," in Tucker and Williams, *Buddhism and Ecology*, 219–48.

75. *ecosteries*   See Alan Drengson, "The Ecostery Foundation of North America: Statement of Philosophy," in *The Trumpeter* 7:1 (winter 1990), 12–16; also Paul Finch, "Combining Technology and Nature on Holy Island," in *The Architects' Journal* (April 18, 1996), 32–37.

75. *Mirabai Bush offers five simple principles*   See Ram Dass and Bush, *Compassion in Action*, 174.

75. *This exercise may help you*   Ram Dass and Bush, *Compassion in Action*, 162–63 (slightly edited).

76. *Upon seeing a bridge*   Taigen Daniel Leighton, *Bodhisattva Archetypes* (New York: Penguin, 1998), 139. The citation is Leighton's paraphrase of the *Avataṃsaka Sutra*.

76. *There is nothing like stepping away from the road*   Snyder, *The Practice of the Wild*, 154.

77. *I stopped meditating*   Nisker, "The Rain Forest as Teacher," 1,6.


AT EASE AMID ACTIVITY

79. *I go out there and just take a deep breath*   Denise Caignon, "Owning the Disowned: A Conversation with Maylie Scott," in *Turning Wheel* (spring 1992), 27.

79. *all buddhas sit in the middle of fire*   Leighton, *Bodhisattva Archetypes*, 141.

79. *Like a fire, a bodhisattva's mind constantly blazes*   Ratnagotravibhāga I, in Conze, *Buddhist Texts Through the Ages*, 130 (slightly edited).

80. *The question is how to engage*   Thich Nhat Hanh, *Living Buddha, Living Christ* (New York: Riverhead Books, 1995), 175.

80. *Find a quiet, comfortable place*   Batchelor, *Buddhism Without Beliefs*, 62–63.

81. *The most activist thing the peace movement*   Robert A. F. Thurman, "Free Lunch Monastery: Uselessness Versus Militarism," in *Inquiring Mind* 13:2 (spring 1997), 22.

81. *Even those of us who are in society*   Sulak Sivaraksa, "Buddhism in a World of Change," in Eppsteiner, *The Path of Compassion*, 11–12.

81. *What's ironic to me*   Cited in Rothberg, "How Straight Is the Spiritual Path?," 38.

82. *My teacher was great in what he said*   Cited in Kapleau, *Awakening to Zen*, 254.

83. *She enjoys her spare moments*   Kazuaki Tanahashi, *Penetrating Laughter: Hakuin's Zen & Art* (Woodstock: Overlook Press, 1984), 66.

83. *How can I get off the wheel?*   Cited in Jack Kornfield, "What Are Skillful Means for Our Time?" in *Inquiring Mind* 14:1 (fall 1997), 10.

SPREADING JOY IN TEN DIRECTIONS

85. *When I live committed like this*   Nisker, "The Rain Forest as Teacher," 7.

85. *In one of my morning meditations*   Gates and Nisker, "Thinking Like Water," 7–8.

86. *attached greater importance to giving*   See Robert E. Buswell, Jr., "The Path to Perdition: The Wholesome Roots and Their Eradication," in Buswell and Gimello, *Paths to Liberation*, 125–26.

86. *as a child at the Zen Center*   Jake Martin and Josh Schrei, "The Sunyata Generation," in *Turning Wheel* (fall 1997), 21.

87. *Here a bodhisattva gives a gift*   Pañcaviṃśatisāhasrikā, in Conze, *Buddhist Texts Through the Ages*, 137.

87. *I feel a deep link between myself and each child*   Thich Nhat Hanh, *The Miracle of Mindfulness*, 57.

89. *There is no way to happiness*   Thich Nhat Hanh, "A Retreat for Environmentalists," Malibu, California, March 1991; audio tape (Berkeley: Parallax Press, 1992).

CODA

90 *the master picked up a tile*   See Kapleau, *The Three Pillars of Zen*, 24–26.

91. *So suggested Tsung-mi*   See Yoshizu Yoshihide, "The Relation between Chinese Buddhist History and Soteriology," in Buswell and Gimello, *Paths to Liberation*, 333.

91. *The Japanese lay Zen teacher Hisamatsu*   See Christopher Ives, *Zen Awakening and Society* (Honolulu: University of Hawaii Press, 1992), 82 and passim.

# Acknowledgments

A project such as this one bears fruit only if many people give generously of their time and expertise. I am deeply grateful to Karen Lawrie, who made vital contributions to the Wheel's structure and imagery at a formative stage. Bodhin Kjolhede perceptively evaluated early sketches, and Thomas Roberts assisted with contractual matters. Stephanie Kaza was an especially demanding and helpful critic. J.C. Brown not only furnished the illustrations; he also offered valuable ideas.

I wish to express my warm appreciation to the following people for reading and commenting insightfully on earlier versions of the text: Elaine Fox, Barbara Hirshkowitz, Deborah Hobler, Eve Kraft, David Raymond, Gilles Richard, Laurence Silberstein, Helen Tworkov, and William Washburn. Special thanks are due to Jeffrey Hunter, who saw the makings of a book in a slim manuscript and then expertly directed the publication process. Finally, I am most indebted to my wife, Trudy, for her good judgment, selfless encouragement, and unending patience.

The "weathermark" identifies this book as a production of Weatherhill, Inc., publishers of fine books on Asia and the Pacific. Editorial supervision: Jeffrey Hunter. Book and cover design: Kellum/McClain. Printing and binding: R.R. Donnelley. The typeface used is Sabon.